PARENTING REDEFINED

PARENTING REDEFINED

A Guide to Understanding and Nurturing Your Child's Behavior to Help Them Thrive

KRISTEN COOK, MD

BLOOMSBURY ACADEMIC
NEW YORK • LONDON • OXFORD • NEW DELHI • SYDNEY

BLOOMSBURY ACADEMIC

Bloomsbury Publishing Inc, 1359 Broadway, New York, NY 10018, USA
Bloomsbury Publishing Plc, 50 Bedford Square, London, WC1B 3DP, UK
Bloomsbury Publishing Ireland, 29 Earlsfort Terrace, Dublin 2, D02 AY28, Ireland

BLOOMSBURY, BLOOMSBURY ACADEMIC and the Diana logo are trademarks of Bloomsbury Publishing Plc

First published in the United States of America 2025

Copyright © Kristen Cook, 2025

Cover design by Jen Huppert
Cover image © istock/TanyaJoy

All rights reserved. No part of this publication may be: i) reproduced or transmitted in any form, electronic or mechanical, including photocopying, recording or by means of any information storage or retrieval system without prior permission in writing from the publishers; or ii) used or reproduced in any way for the training, development or operation of artificial intelligence (AI) technologies, including generative AI technologies. The rights holders expressly reserve this publication from the text and data mining exception as per Article 4(3) of the Digital Single Market Directive (EU) 2019/790.

Bloomsbury Publishing Inc does not have any control over, or responsibility for, any third-party websites referred to or in this book. All internet addresses given in this book were correct at the time of going to press. The author and publisher regret any inconvenience caused if addresses have changed or sites have ceased to exist, but can accept no responsibility for any such changes.

A catalog record for this book is available from the Library of Congress

ISBN: HB: 979-8-88180-811-2
ePDF: 979-8-88186-664-8
eBook: 979-8-88180-812-9

Typeset by Deanta Global Publishing Services, Chennai, India
Printed and bound in the United States of America

For product safety related questions contact productsafety@bloomsbury.com.

To find out more about our authors and books visit www.bloomsbury.com and sign up for our newsletters.

CONTENTS

Acknowledgments viii

Introduction 1

PART I Neurocognitive Development 11

1. Flipping the Script 13
2. Understanding Brain Development: The Basics 17
3. The Fight-Flight-Freeze Response 25
4. Understanding Brain Development: From Toddlers to Teenagers 31
5. The Theory of Cognitive Development 39

PART II Emotional Development 53

6. Understanding Emotions and the Dangers of Emotional Suppression 55
7. The Relationship between Thoughts, Emotions, and Behavior 67
8. Attachment 75

PART III Psychosocial Development 81

9 Modeling 83
10 Psychosocial Development of Infants, Toddlers, and Preschoolers 87
11 Psychosocial Development and the Importance of Play 93
12 Psychosocial Development of Older Children 99

PART IV Temperament 107

13 Understanding Temperament and Goodness of Fit 109
14 Attributes of Temperament 115
15 A Final Word on Temperament 127

PART V Parenting Power Moves 133

16 Putting Development into Practice 135
17 Mission Statements and Family Meetings 145
18 Understanding Common Parenting Misconceptions 153
19 The Importance of Making Mistakes 161

PART VI Discipline 169

20 Understanding Discipline 171
21 Effective Discipline 179

PART VII Parenting: The Struggle Is Real 187

22 Baumrind's Parenting Styles 189
23 The Challenges: Co-Parenting and Parenting Siblings 201

PART VIII Making It Happen 211

24 Discipline Based on Age 213
25 Putting It All Together 225

Notes 229
Bibliography 232
Index 234
About the Author 236

ACKNOWLEDGMENTS

My deepest appreciation and gratitude to all of the families that I have been blessed to provide medical care to throughout the years. Each and every one of you help me learn, you help me grow, and you help me to be a better pediatrician and a better person. I am honored to be a part of your lives, and I thank you for trusting me. It is a joy to watch your children grow and thrive. To my patients who have grown up, had children of your own, and have chosen me to be your children's pediatrician, I cannot express the immense impact that being a multi-generational pediatrician has had, both in my career and in my life. Thank you from the bottom of my heart.

A very special thank you to James Williams, my seventh grade science teacher. Your impact on my life is more profound than you can even imagine. You sparked my love of science, especially in the realm of biology and anatomy. I felt so safe inside your classroom, and I appreciate the fact that we are still in communication thirty years later. I love your photography books and look forward to supporting you at www.inwildlife.com. My hope is that all children have a Mr. Williams somewhere along their academic journey.

To my literary agency, Gray + Miller, I have no words to express my gratitude. Thank you to Scott Jeffery Miller, who took a chance on an unknown woman who reached out to him on Facebook, asking to be mentored. Scott, you believed in me from the start. I appreciate you, Drew Young, Tony Di Costanzo, and everyone else on your team.

My deepest gratitude to Dr. LuAnn Moraski and Dr. Jessica Bowman. Thank you for seeing my potential. Thank you for recognizing how much I was struggling as a first-year resident. Thank you for speaking up and for helping me. I will never forget your kindness and compassion, and I will forever be grateful for your role in saving my career. You are my angels on earth.

Thank you to my mentors in medical school and beyond—Dr. P. J. Malin, Dr. Virginia Aguila, Dr. Theresa Cafaro, and Dr. Margaret Hennessy. By example, you helped me to develop into the pediatrician, and most importantly, the woman I wanted to be. I hope I make you proud.

To my children Mason Thomas and Savannah Rose, my greatest desire for you is that you believe in yourself, treat others with kindness and respect, follow your passions, and use your gifts and talents to make this world a better place. I hope that the guidance provided by me and your dad allow you to become the best version of yourselves, and that you know you are supported and loved no matter what. I love you more than all of the stars in the galaxy.

Last but not least, a huge thanks to my husband, Chad. Thank you for not throwing in the towel in the early years of our relationship when I was in the depths of an eating disorder; when I was over-exercising and abusing laxatives and screaming at you for eating all of the deli turkey in our condo. Thank you for not giving up on me when I was an absolute nightmare to deal with because I was a hungry, anxiety-filled, emotional wreck. Thank you for loving me when I could not even fathom the thought of loving myself. Above all, thank you for supporting me and loving me as I fought for an opportunity to become a better version of myself, without feeling threatened by my progress. Not only did you save my life, you infused it with a renewed purpose. I'm so proud of how far we have come, and I cannot wait to see what life has in store for us in the future.

Introduction

My child is a criminal.

Before I explain why my son should have been put in jail, let me introduce myself. My name is Kristen Cook, MD. I'm a pediatrician with over fifteen years of experience in a thriving medical practice. I graduated from medical school with honors, and I completed a demanding pediatric residency program at one of the best children's hospitals in the United States. I'm also a mom to two amazing, strong-willed children who teach me about life every single day.

I worked full time as a pediatrician for two years before I had my first child. I thought my credentials and expertise would somehow magically turn me into an amazing mom, but I was wrong. As you will soon come to understand, parenting my children successfully was challenging at first. My passion for educating parents about creating more peaceful and effective parenting journeys is why I wrote this book. Let's get back to my criminal son.

My son's first crime occurred at the tender age of two years old. Let me set the scene. Me, my husband, and my son Mason were on vacation. I won't mention the place we were at, but it was a well-known and sought-after vacation destination.

This was a special vacation. It was my son's first trip to a place I have loved for decades, and I wanted it to be perfect. In fact, I was expecting it to be magical. I had spent months planning this trip and had obsessed over every detail. Days were planned to the minute. I even created a color-coded schedule to keep us "on track."

On the day of the crime, we had spent the morning going on rides, and we were getting hungry. We walked into a busy restaurant that happened to be "quick service." Yet the service was anything but quick. While I stood in a very long line to order our food, my husband

and son walked around the restaurant until they were able to secure a corner table. I met them at the table after I placed our order, and we waited for our food to be delivered to us on very fancy red plastic trays with plastic cutlery. When we initially sat down, my son was talking and laughing. As a Mama, I was so proud. We were having such a great vacation!

I'm not sure what happened, but Mason's demeanor immediately changed when the tray of food was placed in front of him. His expression of joy morphed into one of absolute rage. This transformation took nanoseconds, but I had seen it before. My kid was on the verge of turning into a monster. I tried to brace myself for what was about to come next.

I felt as if the world was moving in slow motion. I watched Mason glare at the tray as if it had threatened his very existence. I saw him grab his grilled cheese sandwich, rip it in half, wind up, and fling it as hard as he could. My eyes followed the trajectory of the gooey mess flying through the air, and I could feel my mouth drop open in disbelief. I watched in horror as the right half of the sandwich traveled four tables away, hit its unintended target, and slowly bounced off a man's left cheek. As his facial flesh wiggled and jiggled, I covered my head in embarrassment. Sadly, the incident was far from over.

Mason proceeded to fall on the floor and have a massive temper tantrum. He kicked, he screamed, and he flailed his extremities. Knowing my child, I ignored his behavior and tried to let him work it out. An older woman walked up to our table, looked at Mason, looked at me, looked at Mason again, looked at me (while completely ignoring my husband sitting next to me) and had the audacity to proclaim, "If he was my kid, I'd raise him right!" At the time, her words stung worse than a slap across the face. I felt defeated and like a total failure as a parent.

Instead of spiraling into self-deprecation, I did a deep dive into the situation. Over the next few days, I reflected on the aspects that led up to the grilled cheese debacle. Could the situation have been prevented? Was there something that I could have done differently? How could I help my son regulate his behavior in the future? For the rest of the trip, I observed the actions of both children and their parents. I witnessed so many temper tantrums, and so many arguments, during that vacation. This sparked a desire to learn as much as I could about neuroscience, child development, discipline, and parent-child relationships. I'd like to share that information with you.

If you have ever been frustrated, confused, or completely embarrassed by your child's behavior, you are not alone. I don't know a single parent who has not felt the exact same way! Being a parent is by far the hardest, yet most rewarding job on planet. Yet the behaviors that our children demonstrate can come across as mean, hurtful, and downright embarrassing. At times, my kids act in ways that make me not want to be around them. I bet yours do too. Please understand that there is nothing wrong with you, and there is nothing wrong with your child.

Your kids did not come into this world with a mission to make your life as difficult as possible. They do not intentionally act in ways that perpetuate your stress or embarrassment on a regular basis. In fact, your kids love you deeply and rely on your guidance more than you could ever imagine. They crave your attention. They long for connection with you, even when their actions seem to indicate otherwise.

Why do our kids misbehave while simultaneously vying for our love and affection? The simple answer is that many of those unwanted behaviors are biologically driven. In most cases, your child is not intentionally trying to misbehave. There are deep-seated, evolutionary factors involved. Quite simply, your child misbehaves when their brain becomes overwhelmed. A lot of problematic behaviors that children engage in are simply an expression of an overwhelmed brain.

To make matters more complicated, as parents, we have not been taught the importance of understanding the world from our child's perspective. Rather, we have been taught that we know better, because we are the adults. We are often told that certain parenting strategies are recommended based on their processes and procedures. However, trying to mold our children to fit a particular parenting strategy will fail. This is because in most cases, parents have not been provided with the information that they need to truly understand and effectively parent the unique child or children that they are blessed to raise. Until now.

The disconnect is in the history of our species as human beings. As we will discover, societal attitudes about children and parenting have varied greatly throughout history. Yet, throughout history, parents have been led to believe that they must control their children. Unfortunately, this premise causes parents to adopt ineffective ideologies and to act in certain ways that are detrimental to future generations. Certainly, as parents, we do not intend to be detrimental. I firmly believe that we do what we do until we know how to do better. Yet, often our experiences and struggles create further disconnect.

To make matters worse, outside influences are constantly bombarding us with information and, more commonly, misinformation. We are "supposed" to do this and we are "never" to do that. Seemingly well-intentioned friends and relatives provide unsolicited advice on a regular basis. Any online search will yield conflicting and often ineffective strategies related to parenting and discipline. For the moms, we face the additional pressure to do all things, be everything to everyone, and look good while we are doing it.

I cannot tell you how many parents I have counseled over the years about sleep problems, temper tantrums, biting, back talk, and so much more. It's in the tens of thousands. As a pediatrician with a diverse patient population, I provide care for patients from a wide variety of socioeconomic backgrounds. Yet, many of the parenting struggles are the same. My advice to my families has been this:

> *You need to parent the child that you have, rather than the child you wish you had.*

I want you to read that statement again, with an open mind. If you have ever told your child, "Stop crying!" you are not parenting the child you have. If you have ever expected your five-year-old to get ready for bed and brush their teeth without a single reminder, you are not parenting the child you have. If you have ever forced your child to participate in a sport that they do not like, you are not parenting the child you have.

Furthermore, if you have multiple children, each of them will require a slightly different parenting strategy. You will have a much more peaceful and effective parenting journey if you parent each child that you have, right here and right now. If you are willing to understand your child and meet them where they are instead of where you want them to be, parenting will become much less stressful and much more enjoyable. It sounds simple, but in reality, this concept is very complex.

I need you to understand that this approach has nothing to do with love. I have no doubt that you love your child or children fiercely. I believe that you want the best for them and are doing the best that you can. Yet, as a mom and a pediatrician, I know that you have not been provided with the information that you need to parent the child that you have—until now.

In order to understand your children and parent them to the best of your ability, you need a specific skill set. You need to understand the human brain and how it develops. You need to understand the basics of social and emotional development. You need to understand the concept of temperament and use that information to determine your child's unique temperament. You need to learn how to implement effective discipline instead of punishment. If that sounds overwhelming, please do not worry. I will walk you through it, one step at a time. All you need to do is commit to understanding your child where they are at, and parent them in a way that understands and accepts their view of themselves and of the world around them.

When I finally was able to get pregnant with a viable pregnancy (my first pregnancy ended in a miscarriage), I was ecstatic. I had wanted to become a mom for so long, and finally my dream was coming true. When I was pregnant with my son, I read the "best" parenting books. I bought a lot of stuff that I thought I needed. I talked to my esteemed colleagues about their parenting experiences. I made my non-physician husband practice changing diapers on a teddy bear. I thought I did everything to prepare myself for motherhood.

Remember, I thought that my experience as a pediatrician with a thriving medical practice would help me effortlessly transition into my role as a mom. I was very, very wrong.

When my son was born, I was like most moms. I had a desire to do everything "right." Yet, parenting my son was really hard. He was born premature and had to be hospitalized for a week after he was born. He spent days in an isolette (an enclosed crib made of clear plastic that maintains a warm environment) under phototherapy lights, with limited ability to be held. He developed infantile colic, which was a nightmare. He had acid reflux disease. For months, he wore a helmet twenty-three hours a day to correct his flat head. He needed four surgeries before the age of two. He hated sleep from the day he was born. Despite my intense love for him, he was an extremely challenging infant.

I constantly felt like I was failing him. I was riddled with guilt and shame and embarrassment because of my perceived parenting flaws. Doing the things that were recommended to me by my child's pediatrician, social media parenting groups, as well as friends and relatives were not helpful. Parenting my son was still a struggle.

Over time, I realized that a lot of my frustrations were based on unrealistic expectations that I had of my son. I wanted him to sleep through the night (which he did not do consistently until he was six years old). I wanted him to never throw a massive temper tantrum in public (which he did often as a toddler). I wished he didn't need surgery (which was out of everyone's control).

My daughter was very different. She was born full term. We went home from the hospital two days after she was born. She didn't have infantile colic, or a need for a helmet, and she has yet to undergo a surgical procedure. She was calmer than my son, had an easier time going to sleep, and overall was easier to soothe. This dichotomy piqued my interest. My son and daughter have the same parents. At the time, they were raised in a similar manner. So why were they so different?

These differences fueled me to develop an even deeper interest in neuroscience, child development, and parenting skills—more so than the fateful vacation with my criminal toddler. I have sought additional training in these fields in order to be a more effective parent and a more knowledgeable and helpful pediatrician. Do I have a PhD in neuroscience? Nope. But I am confident in my abilities to help others understand the information needed to be a highly successful parent.

I'll be the first to admit that parenting my daughter is much easier than parenting my son. That does not mean that my daughter is somehow better than my son! Easier does not equate to better. My children are two different people with unique personalities and temperaments. I love them both equally and fiercely. But as human beings, they each deserve the best of my ability to be their mom. I have learned to tailor my parenting skills based on my child's needs. In the upcoming chapters, I will teach you how to do this as well. Before I do that, I need to take you on a journey back in time.

In order to create a better future for ourselves and for our children, we need to understand the past. Most parents don't take the time to evaluate where their beliefs about parenting and discipline have come from, or how those strategies could be improved. I encourage you to become aware. Take some time to think about your parenting. Where did your current views about children and parenting come from, and how have those views evolved over time?

Are you ready for something that seems completely unfathomable? Infanticide, or the intentional killing of infants, appears to have been a common practice in some societies. Often, it was used as a method to dispose of unwanted infants—infants who had birth defects, were born out of wedlock, or, most commonly, who were a financial burden to their families. In numerous societies throughout history, infants were left to die by exposure. These were babies who were abandoned in nature and subsequently died from hypothermia, starvation, dehydration, or animal attack.

In some cultures, infanticide may have been even more deliberate. In ancient Sparta, a group of elders assessed each child shortly after they were born. If the infant had physical deformities or were deemed unhealthy, they were thrown off a cliff. In China, female infants were drowned simply because of their sex. In India, female infants were often considered an unwanted expense and killed because of the dowry system. In ancient Japan, the opposite was the case. Female children were spared because they could be sold off as servants, prostitutes, or sent to become geishas.

Fortunately, the practice of infanticide is almost unheard of today. However, historical attitudes toward children were very different than they are today. It was not until recently that children were valued for simply being kids. For centuries, children were expected to work in order to support their families. As little as two hundred years ago, children were exploited on a regular basis. For example, during the American Industrial Revolution, children as young as three years old were sent to work outside of their homes. They worked long hours in coal mines or mills under dangerous conditions and for terrible wages. These children experienced stunted growth, malnutrition, and even physical abuse during their working hours.

Child maltreatment was not limited to the Industrial Revolution. Even prominent pediatricians encouraged practices that are unheard of today. In 1894, Dr. Luther Holt published a book called *The Care and Feeding of Children*, in which he advocated for regimented and strict parenting.[1] He advised inflexible schedules for eating and toilet training, and claimed that playing with babies under the age of six months soon after feeding caused them to become nervous, irritable, and suffer from indigestion. He also claimed that children who liked sweets did so because they had an "indulgent" parent.

How about infants with colic? Infantile colic is a condition where children are inconsolable for hours on end. There is a biological basis for this behavior, which was not understood at the time. In the late 1800s, infants with colic were supposed to be held in front of an open fire. If that didn't cure their colic, they were supposed to be given an enema of half a warm teacup of water with ten drops of turpentine oil in it. Turpentine oil used in this manner can cause kidney damage, brain damage, and even death. Yet Dr. Holt's book was considered the gold standard of parenting advice for decades.

In 1928, psychologist John B. Watson published the book *Psychological Care of Infant and Child*, and it soon became a favorite among parents. Watson recommended,

> Let your behavior always be objective and kindly firm. Never hug and kiss them, never let them sit in your lap. If you must, kiss them once on the forehead when they say good night. Shake hands with them in the morning. Give them a pat on the head if they have made an extraordinarily good job of a difficult task.[2]

I am not introducing you to this historical information in order to be critical. I don't want you, or anyone else, to judge these people who were considered experts in their field. I simply want you to understand that as parents, we do what we know until we know how to do better. In the late 1800s, parents who followed the advice of Dr. Holt were considered amazing parents!

If we are committed to being open-minded and to learning new things, we are on the path to becoming more informed and effective parents. We can learn from our collective past in order to do better in the future. Past generations were not inclined to understand the behavior of their kids. Yet this understanding can transform our experience as parents and can change the trajectory of our children's futures.

PART I

NEUROCOGNITIVE DEVELOPMENT

1

Flipping the Script

Almost every single challenging or frustrating behavior that your child has ever demonstrated is the result of one single, indisputable biological fact. Are you ready for it? Drumroll please . . . a child's brain is under construction. No matter their age, a child's brain is not fully developed. The human brain does not fully develop until a person is in their mid-twenties. Kids cannot think like adults, which is why they do not, and cannot, act like adults. This is a biological fact. Their brain is not fully developed, and yours is. You cannot expect your child to act in the same manner that you act. I need you to embrace this concept, regardless of what you have been taught in the past.

In addition, kids lack perspective. They cannot adopt someone else's point of view to the same degree that you, with a fully developed brain, are able to. Your child needs to learn how to view the world through someone else's eyes, and this type of learning takes time. As a parent, you need to be patient. You need to develop an understanding of what your child is capable of in the present moment.

Your child cannot interact with the world around them in the same manner that you interact with the world around you. Your life as a parent will be so much easier if you commit to trying to view the world through your child's eyes. Attempting to view the world in the same manner that your child views the world will help you understand their actions on a completely different level. This will allow you to respond to their behavior in a more effective and impactful manner.

Let me give you an example. It's lunchtime. You are at work and you are hungry. You open your lunchbox to find leftovers that you don't have a taste for. Ick. You subconsciously realize that you have a choice. You can eat the unwanted leftovers, or you can walk over to the cafeteria to buy a different meal instead of eating food that you don't have a taste for. You utilize the skills of problem-solving and judgment to make such a decision without even realizing it. You buy and eat your cafeteria food and go about your day without incident.

Your toddler, on the other hand, does not possess the critical-thinking skills of an adult. When she opens her lunchbox and finds leftovers that she does not have a taste for, she has a different response. Her brain does not realize that she can ask her teacher for a different lunch. Worse yet, her brain perceives those leftovers as threatening. In the upcoming chapters, we will learn why that food was perceived as a threat. Let's get back to your toddler's response. She yells and throws her lunch across the room. She proceeds to have a temper tantrum because she is hungry, frustrated, and lacks the verbal skills to express her wants and needs.

I empathize with that child's temper tantrum. While I understand the behavior, I also understand that it is undesired. I consider undesired childhood behavior to be an expression of an overwhelmed brain, especially in the pre-teenage years. I encourage you to adopt a similar perspective.

When your child behaves in an undesired manner, it is because their brain is not fully developed. Acknowledge that the development of the human brain takes many years to complete, and commit to understanding your child's brain. If you can understand what your child's brain is and is not capable of, you will have a better understanding of their behavior. Understanding this sets the foundation for helping your child learn to behave more appropriately in the future.

At birth, all the major parts of the brain are intact. In fact, we are born with approximately the same number of neurons (or brain cells) that we have when we die. However, the appropriate neural pathways, meaning the connections between different neurons, need time to develop. The human brain is constantly wiring and rewiring itself based upon a person's interactions with other people and with the world around them. It is continuously creating and destroying new highways. The paths that are traveled the most grow strong. The paths that get dusty may eventually be torn down. This is a process called pruning.

Let's take a trip down memory lane. Do you remember when your child was an infant? You loved seeing your child's developmental skills emerge. You were excited to hear their first word. You waited with anticipation for them to start walking, and you cheered like crazy when those shaky steps first emerged. You couldn't wait for your child to be able to play catch, or to sing the entire chorus of "Twinkle, Twinkle Little Star."

During this point in your child's life, you loved your child's immature brain, even if you weren't aware of it. You relished every new accomplishment, every new skill. You probably recorded it in a baby book or as a reminder on your cell phone. For most parents, this appreciation of the immature brain was unconscious. Initially, your child's underdeveloped brain was a source of joy. There is nothing wrong with that! I want you to be able to recognize this, and own it, because these milestones are wonderful and precious.

I need you to understand that your child's developing brain only became a problem when your child's behavior became undesirable.

Read that statement again, and please understand that there is no judgment in it. There is a subtle transition between enjoying our baby's behaviors and dreading our toddler's behaviors. You probably didn't mind changing poopy diapers in the beginning, even though they seemed to be never-ending. Yet, as your child got older, you couldn't fathom why they ran to a corner to poop in their diaper instead of pooping on the potty. You probably thought it was cute when your baby chewed on their banana toothbrush, yet struggled when your toddler resisted your attempts to brush their teeth.

You look at the world with your (assumingly) fully developed brain and your child does not. Furthermore, your child is not capable of understanding your view of the world. Again, this means that the ways in which you perceive and react to the world around you are going to be very different the ways in which your child perceives and reacts to the world around them.

Remember the leftovers example. The exact same situation perceived by two very different brains will inevitably lead to two different outcomes. Your child may not be able to understand your view of the world, but your fully developed brain has the capacity to understand your child's view. As a parent, you have two choices: (1) You can choose to ignore biological facts and continue to parent your child your way. This will likely lead to a lot of frustration, the creation of unreasonable standards, and kids who eventually grow up to resent you, fail to live up to their potential, or both. Sorry to be blunt, but I have seen this occur time and time again in my pediatric medical practice. (2) Or, you can sit with the idea that changing your expectations based on your child's physical, emotional, and social skills may help both you and your child have a more peaceful and fulfilling life.

The choice is yours, and I hope you choose the latter. Think about how amazing it would be if you could understand your child's brain. If you could understand why your child acts the way that they do. Even better, once you gain an understanding of these things, how amazing would it be to help your child act in a more positive, less problematic manner?

2

Understanding Brain Development
The Basics

I strongly believe that every single parent would benefit from having a basic understanding of how the nervous system works and how it develops. The nervous system includes the brain and spinal cord, as well as the nerves that transmit information throughout the body. Understanding how the nervous system, and particularly the brain, develops can have profound impacts on parenting behaviors. I alluded to this in a previous chapter and now it's time for a detailed explanation.

The cells of the nervous system are called neurons. The connections between neurons are called synapses. Synapses allow brain cells to communicate with each other. I like to think of neurons as destinations on a map. They are restaurants, stores, parks, and homes. The synaptic connections are the roads that connect those destinations.

As the brain develops, certain synaptic pathways will strengthen, and others will weaken and eventually be destroyed. The more a neural pathway is used, the stronger the likelihood that the pathway will continue to develop. The more the pathway is used, the stronger it will become. A pathway that is deemed unnecessary will be destroyed in a process called pruning. However, these processes are dependent on experience. Life experiences will cause the brain to change and adapt. This is a concept called neuroplasticity.

The strength of the pathway results in the storage of information. Stored information results in behavioral outcomes. As parents, we need to help strengthen the synaptic pathways that help our children learn to thrive. How we do that successfully will be discussed in future chapters. For now, we stick with the basics.

It's important to understand that brain development begins in utero. It is essential for pregnant women to receive adequate prenatal care and to take good care of themselves during pregnancy. Proper nutrition, exercise, and taking the medically recommended vitamins are important. So is avoiding alcohol, nicotine-containing products such as cigarettes and e-cigarettes, and drugs including marijuana.

There is a great deal of information regarding fetal alcohol syndrome, which results from excessive alcohol use during pregnancy. There is increasing evidence regarding the negative impact of marijuana on the fetal brain; just like alcohol, it can cause permanent brain damage. In my experience, women often turn toward marijuana to manage pregnancy-related nausea. This can potentially lead to problems within the developing fetus. Based on my experiences, behavioral problems and difficult-to-control ADHD symptoms have been associated with marijuana use during pregnancy. In fact, there is emerging research that supports my observations. Prenatal cannabis use has been associated with an increased risk of ADHD as well as autism spectrum disorders.[1]

The brain develops from back to front and inside out. The physical structure of the brain is amazingly complex, but let's keep it simple. I like to think of the human brain as being composed of three main structures: the hindbrain, the midbrain, and the forebrain. The hindbrain is the most primitive part of the brain. It includes the cerebellum, pons, and medulla oblongata. The hindbrain regulates functions that keep us alive. It controls heart rate, breathing, sleeping, and movement, among other things. It also connects the brain to the spinal cord.

The midbrain is composed of the tegmentum and the tectum, which are made up of a bunch of small parts with long names. The midbrain helps to relay information that is essential for vision and hearing. It controls most of our eye movement. It plays a role in the sensation of pain and temperature, response to fear, and modulates the sleep-wake cycle.

The functions of the hindbrain and midbrain are largely involuntary, meaning that we have little control over them. While these portions of the brain are essential, they don't necessarily help us with parenting. I thank them for their contributions to our survival as humans and appreciate their functions. However, in this book, the focus will be on the forebrain, the largest portion of the human brain. The forebrain is divided into two parts: the neocortex and the limbic system.

The limbic system is the lower, more primitive portion of the forebrain. It governs important aspects of emotion, motivation, and rewards. It is involved with long-term memory. Furthermore, the limbic system is responsible for the fight-flight-freeze response. When it comes to parenting, the most important thing to understand about the limbic system is that it is emotional and reactive.

The neocortex is the higher portion of the forebrain, both physically and metaphorically. It is a structure that is unique to mammals. The neocortex is the portion of the brain that takes the longest to fully develop. It is composed of four lobes—frontal, temporal, parietal, and occipital—as well as a structure called the corpus callosum.

I know that this information is complex. Let me offer a brief recap. The hindbrain and the midbrain are out of our conscious awareness. I mention them for completeness. We'll focus on the parts of the brain that we can control in the forebrain.

Yet there is a catch when it comes to the forebrain. The functions of the limbic system, the lower portion of the neocortex, are also out of our conscious awareness. This means that emotionality and reactiveness will be the default response unless we intentionally decide to be rational. The functions of the neocortex are within our conscious awareness. This will be an important distinction in upcoming chapters.

By the way, I understand that this information is technical and dry. Close your eyes and take a few deep breaths if you need to. I want to be thorough, but I also want to focus on brain development as it relates to parenting.

The neocortex has a lot of responsibilities. It regulates conscious thought, information processing, voluntary movement, and personality. Possibly one of the most intriguing aspects of the neocortex is something called executive functioning skills, which are governed by the frontal lobes of the brain.

Executive functioning skills help us to achieve goals. I understand that this seems vague, but this is because anything that relates to decision-making, time management, and holding information in our memory in order to use that information involves executive functioning skills. There are seven executive functioning skills:

- Emotional regulation
- Inhibition (impulse control and self-restraint)
- Planning and problem-solving
- Self-awareness
- Nonverbal working memory (short-term memory related to senses, time, and mental images)
- Verbal working memory (such as self-talk)
- Motivational regulation

Executive skills are some of the final cognitive skills to develop. Even legal adults, at eighteen years old, do not possess these skills fully! How does this relate to parenting? This knowledge can help us to understand that young children lack inhibition, and thus are often impulsive. It can help us to understand that children feel big emotions, yet lack the ability to express those emotions in a socially appropriate manner. It can help us to understand why a child does not complete a task that we have asked them to perform.

Children need to learn skills such as the ability to plan, remember instructions, pay attention for sustained periods of time, multitask, and think before they act. These are skills that develop over time as the brain continues to develop. The capacity to use reasoning, or to think about something in a logical way, is a higher order executive functioning skill. It requires several basic executive functioning skills to work together. It's safe to assume that the younger your child, the more irrational they will be.

Children are born with the capacity to learn executive functioning skills, and this type of learning takes time.

To make matters more complicated, when faced with a challenge, the brain will look toward the path of least resistance. The path of least resistance is often the strongest synaptic connection. This means that the brain will default to what it knows best in attempts to solve a problem. The synaptic pathways that have been used the most will be the first to respond.

Which means that reactive, emotional, and explosive behaviors are the norm when your kids are preschoolers and toddlers, and sometimes even for school-age children and teenagers. The human brain is wired for efficiency, and brain efficiency is directly correlated to synaptic pathways.

Efficiency is the reason a toddler will scream, "I hate you!" when they are mad. Has your child said that to you yet? If not, it's coming. My daughter was only four years old when she first told me that she hated me. She didn't gently say that phrase; she screamed it at me while she slammed her bedroom door in my face. Fun times.

Seriously though, how many times have you as an adult screamed "I hate you!" at your boss? Probably never, no matter how many times you think it, because your neocortex steps in to make you think twice before you open your mouth. As a fully grown adult, you have the benefit of life experiences that have strengthened positive synaptic connections. Your neocortex is fully developed and allows you to act in a (mostly) rational manner.

I want you to think about a time when someone did something that caused you to feel angry. Let's say that you have just given an important presentation at work. You worked overtime without extra pay on this particular project. It is something that you are passionate about, and you truly believe that the information in this presentation will take your company to the next level. Instead of providing support, your boss decides to trash your presentation in front of every single executive in the room. You are angry, mortified, and disappointed all at the same time.

Your instinct is to either yell at your boss and tell him what a jerk he is, run out of the room in embarrassment, or attempt to hide under the table. These are the fight-flight-freeze responses of the limbic system, which will be discussed in detail in the next chapter. Yet you do none of these, because your neocortex takes over. Your brain unconsciously whispers to you: "Whoa, slow down, think about what you are going to do before you do it." Instead of doing something that may get you fired, you muster a smile, thank the executives, and calmly walk back to your office. You may hit your desk or throw a pen, but you do so in your office, in private. Again, you can thank your frontal lobes for this.

Finally, regardless of someone's age or developmental abilities, please understand that the human brain needs to know what to do. Telling it what not to do is not helpful. Yet this is a common approach among parents. How many times have you told your child, "Don't do that!" or "Don't touch that!"?

Let me help you understand why this is ineffective. Have you ever told yourself not to cry? I bet you sobbed. Have you ever told yourself not to eat the cookies in the break room at work? I bet you ate three of them. Again, the human brain needs to understand what to do. Telling it what not to do is ineffective.

In the book *The Whole-Brain Child* by Daniel J. Siegel, MD, and Tina Payne Bryson, PhD, the human brain is likened to a house with an "upstairs brain" and a "downstairs brain."[2] The downstairs brain is the primitive, reactive portion of the brain where all the essential functions occur. The upstairs brain is the neocortex, where the advanced activities occur. This is an amazing concept, and I highly recommend this book, but I like to think about it in a slightly different way.

I see the neocortex as a coach and the limbic system as the student. The neocortex is a former professional musician who has become a music teacher. She has experience, skill, and talent that developed over many years. Her new student is the limbic system, a child who only recently developed a love for playing the cello. This child oozes with potential but lacks the thousands of hours of practice that the musician has already put into her trade. The child easily gets frustrated when playing a wrong note.

Parents, you are that music teacher. You have a fully developed neocortex and are fully capable of helping your child's neocortex to develop. If you understand your little cello player and what they are and are not capable of today, right here and right now, you can help them to create beautiful music one day.

3

The Fight-Flight-Freeze Response

One of my favorite parts of the limbic system is the amygdala. The amygdala is a tiny, almond-shaped structure. The amygdala regulates the fight-flight-freeze response. When faced with a threat, the human body has seconds to prepare itself to fight the threat, run away from the threat (i.e., flight) or freeze in terror.

The amygdala is responsible for helping our physical bodies to respond to threats. A threat does not even need to be real; a perceived threat will trigger the exact same unconscious biological response. This concept is especially important when it comes to parenting. A threat is a threat, even if it is not real.

From an evolutionary standpoint, the fight-flight-freeze response was essential for survival. It helped us live through dangerous and potentially deadly situations. The classic example is that of a prehistoric human being confronted by a saber-tooth tiger. In order to survive, the human brain needed to decide very quickly if the human should run away from the tiger or stay and fight, as freezing would inevitably lead to death. That decision is below the level of our consciousness.

The fight-flight-freeze response involves an amazingly complex release of hormones and chemical messengers that lead to action (or inaction). The heart rate speeds up. The pupils dilate. Blood flow to the major muscle groups increases. The perception of pain temporarily decreases. When your body senses that something is dangerous, this response will be automatic. Just because we live in a civilized society does not mean that the fight-flight-freeze response has gone away. They may be extinct, but the human brain is still on the lookout for all those saber-tooth tigers!

Modern-day saber-tooth tigers are very real and threaten us multiple times per day; they just appear in different forms. For adults, traffic jams, deadlines at work, financial problems, and watching your child run into the street without looking for cars are all examples of threats. For kids, a piece of broccoli, being asked to share a toy, or being benched during a basketball game may be threatening. Remember, threats do not have to be real in order to activate the fight-flight-freeze response.

I want you to try to identify the modern saber-tooth tigers in your child's life. What threats does your child come across that activate their fight-flight-freeze response? And remember, those threats may not pose an actual threat to survival. It's all about perception.

Why is this important? Because identifying those threats not only deepens your understanding of your unique child, it can help you to create a game plan to avoid triggers. You can help prevent your child from going into fight-flight-freeze mode. For example, if you know that your child will have a meltdown if he has to wear a shirt that has a tag, you can cut the tag out.

Furthermore, it's important to understand that perceived threats may change over time. One week, a piece of broccoli may be perceived as a threat and result in fight-mode-induced throwing and yelling. The next week, broccoli may be accepted, and suddenly watermelon is perceived as a threat. This is particularly true for toddlers and preschoolers.

When my son was three years old, he caused another child to sustain a concussion because of his amygdala-driven fight response. At the time, I worked for a large healthcare organization, and we were fortunate to have an on-site daycare for children of employees. My son had been attending that daycare since he was seven weeks old. It was a close-knit community, and many of the teachers had become like family to us. When Mason was a toddler, his class was outside for recess.

They were playing with chalk. Apparently, another child stole the chalk right out of Mason's hand. Mason responded by pushing the child in attempts to get his chalk back. That child stumbled, fell backward onto the asphalt, hit his head, and ended up developing a concussion.

I felt awful. Yet numerous teachers, as well as the director of the daycare, reassured me that my son was not acting maliciously. He did not intend to hurt the other child. His brain perceived a threat, and he went into fight-flight-freeze mode. As is common with many toddlers, the fight mode prevailed.

As parents, we cannot magically turn off our child's fight-flight-freeze response. In fact, we cannot turn off our own fight-flight-freeze response. However, as human beings with fully developed brains, we have the advantage of being able to use our frontal lobes to override this biologically driven response. Children, especially toddlers and young school-age children, can't tap into their frontal lobes in the same way that we can.

So, the next time your child throws their dinner on the floor and proceeds to sob uncontrollably, recognize that their food was threatening. The next time your child pushes their sibling for taking their doll, understand that they are reacting to someone who is intruding on their turf. The next time your child throws a massive temper tantrum in the grocery store, recognize that the intent was not to embarrass you.

This does not mean that you need to accept their behavior and encourage it to continue. This would be detrimental to your child's development. Rather, developing an awareness of the problematic behavior can help you manage it in a more effective manner.

The fight-flight-freeze response is necessary for survival, and people of all ages and developmental stages experience it. Understanding the behaviors that are a result of the fight-flight-freeze response does not mean that we accept them or normalize them. Biology does not mean that discipline goes out the window. Certainly, if your child pushes their sibling, they need to be disciplined in developmentally appropriate ways. We will learn about this soon. Again, for now, we are focused on understanding.

Problematic Behavior and Its Relation to the Amygdala

Problematic behavior has a number of definitions, but for the purposes of this book, problematic behavior will refer to behaviors that children demonstrate that most parents would find to be unacceptable or unwanted, despite any biological explanation for that behavior. Examples include temper tantrums, back talk, acting out aggressively, lying, picky eating, smoking marijuana, and having unprotected sex.

I want you to view problematic behavior in younger children as an expression of the fight-flight-freeze response. When your child acts out in ways that you do not like, it is usually because their amygdala has taken over. Remember, when faced with a threat, the human body automatically and unconsciously releases a flood of chemical messages in order to prepare the body to fight, run away, or freeze.

Let's go through some examples. Imagine that you are the parent of four-year-old Grace. You decide to have a playdate for Grace and invite her friend Avery over to your home. This is the first time that Avery has been over, and Grace seems very excited to play with her. Grace and Avery are doing great until Avery happens to pick up Grace's favorite doll and give it a big snuggle. Grace responds by pushing Avery and taking her doll back.

You are horrified, but Grace just demonstrated a fight response. Her brain perceived someone stealing her favorite baby, and she fought to get it back. She was not intentionally trying to be mean to Avery. She was not trying to hurt Avery. Her behavior was a manifestation of a biologically driven response. Her turf was invaded, and she was staking her claim.

Next, imagine that you are the parent of seven-year-old Max. Like most kids, Max is famished when he gets home from school. You make him a quick snack, then turn your attention to the three baskets of laundry that are waiting for you. The next time you walk into the kitchen, you catch Max with his hand in the cookie jar. You had previously told him that cookies were off-limits before dinner and reminded him of this fact when you catch him red-handed. He instantly stops moving, with a hand full of Oreos. This is an expression of a freeze response.

Your three-year-old did not throw a temper tantrum because they are an asshole. Your six-year-old did not refuse to eat the stuffed peppers you made for dinner because they are intent on being defiant. Your eight-year-old did not lie about doing their homework because they intentionally wanted to see you get upset. The brains of kids are not that sophisticated. It takes frontal lobe abilities to intentionally choose to behave in a way that is going to piss their parents off, and younger children do not have such cognitive abilities.

When your child acts in a manner that you do not like, they are not intentionally trying to be uncooperative, difficult, or defiant. In fact, their behavior is not about you at all! It stems from a biologically driven and unconscious process. As parents, with time, we can help our children learn how to modulate this response.

I'd like to help you avoid an approach that will absolutely backfire when it comes to managing problematic behavior.

Many parents try to talk their child out of expressing a problematic behavior in the moment when that behavior is actually occurring. This . . . will . . . backfire. If your child's fight-flight-freeze response has kicked in, there is nothing that you or your developed brain can do to stop their behavior. I promise, you cannot talk your child out of this mode. Once a person has succumbed to fight-flight-freeze mode, there is no way out other than to go through it. As a parent, you need to step back, stop talking, and let your child's nervous system calm down on its own.

This is so important that I am going to write it again, in a slightly different way. You cannot use reason to stop a behavior that is the result of the fight-flight-freeze response. Your attempts will be perceived as an additional threat, and the behavior will actually get worse. Please let that sink in. You will make the situation worse by trying to reason with someone who is in the middle of a fight-flight-freeze response.

Instead of responding, give your child the time and space to let themselves self-regulate, whatever that may look like. They may scream and pound their fists and thrash around on the floor. That's okay. They may throw food, or cry, or grab a toy and rock back and forth. Take a step away, be quiet, but remain within your child's line of vision. Resist the urge to respond until your child has calmed down.

Problematic behavior eventually ends. The tantrum resolves, the kicking stops, the toy is returned to its rightful owner. Rather than taking that behavior at face value, recognize the behavior for what it is, which is an unconscious expression of an emotional and reactive brain. In upcoming chapters, you will learn how to discipline these unwanted expressions of the fight-flight-freeze response. Staying calm, allowing your child to self-regulate, and briefly explaining future desired behaviors are at the core of this discipline strategy. I will describe this in detail later. For now, we'll focus on the neurocognitive development of children, from toddlers to teenagers.

4

Understanding Brain Development

From Toddlers to Teenagers

Neurocognitive Development of Toddlers and Preschoolers

I want you to understand that toddlers are emotional and reactive. Their limbic system is in charge, because their neocortex is far from fully developed. This is why they tend to engage in problematic behaviors such as temper tantrums, picky eating, and toilet training refusal. It's important to understand that toddlers and preschoolers do not misbehave with the intention to upset their parents. Quite honestly, their brain is not developed enough to employ such a sophisticated strategy. They misbehave because their brain becomes overwhelmed, and they lack the skills to effectively communicate their needs.

In the previous chapter, I discussed the fight-flight-freeze response. Please understand that this response is at the core of the majority of toddler and preschooler behavior. Let's go through a few examples.

You are the parent to three-year-old Hannah. She loves to go to the park and swing on the swings. She happens to have a favorite swing, which is currently occupied by another child. Hannah storms over to the child on "her" swing and demands that the other child leave immediately. Hannah is forceful and unkind in her request. As a parent, you are concerned about Hannah's disrespectful behavior.

From a neurocognitive perspective, Hannah views the swing as her own. It doesn't matter that the swing is public property; according to Hannah, the swing should be available to her when she wants it. If someone else is on "her" swing, her turf has been invaded. Hannah immediately goes into fight mode, and a confrontation ensues.

Hannah's fight response prevailed because her brain is not developed enough to nicely ask the other child to share the swing. Her brain is not developed enough to understand that all swings at the park are similar, and each can provide a fun experience.

Let's go through one more example. You are feeding your two-year-old son Ethan. You place a small amount of well-cut strawberries on his plate. This is a fruit he has seemed to enjoy for the past few weeks. Yet today, he looks at those strawberries, picks them up, and flings them across the kitchen. He proceeds to scream and bang his head repeatedly on his high chair.

For whatever reason, Ethan viewed the strawberries as a threat to his very existence. His fight mode kicked in, and he did what he needed to do to get those strawberries as far away from him as possible.

I know what you may be thinking. Do toddlers and preschoolers always react with a fight response? What about flight or freeze? A fight response occurs when a child is comfortable in their environment. A freeze response tends to occur when a child is frightened. This is the case of a toddler or preschooler who is subjected to yelling on a repeated basis. I will discuss yelling in greater detail in later chapters. When a child is young, if they are yelled at, they will freeze. This may temporarily pause an unwanted behavior, but yelling is never a great solution.

What about the flight response? Have you ever watched a toddler run to a corner or behind a couch to poop in their diaper instead of in the toilet? That's a flight response.

How do we as parents utilize this information to help our children stop throwing strawberries? Or learn how to swing on a different swing?

It's a three-step process. Step number 1 is to remain calm when your child misbehaves. Don't worry, I will discuss strategies to stay calm in upcoming chapters. Step 2 is to step back and allow your child to self-regulate. Do not address your child until they are completely calm. It may take them twenty minutes to calm down. That's okay. You cannot talk your child out of a temper tantrum. You cannot stop your child from flinging food across the room. Let them calm themselves down. Step 3 is to debrief the unwanted behavior. Briefly acknowledge your child's emotions. Explain how their behavior was undesired. Finally, describe a preferred future behavior.

Let's go through an example. You are the parent to three-year-old Aaron, whom you took to the grocery store to pick up a few items. He asks for a large candy bar, and you decline. He proceeds to have a temper tantrum in the middle of aisle 7. Aaron is writhing around on the floor, kicking and screaming about the candy bar he needs to have. Despite any onlookers, you remain calm. Aaron's tantrum eventually ends, and he looks up at you. You get down to his level, look him in the eyes and say, "Gosh it looks like you were angry. But throwing yourself on the floor is not okay. Can you ask mom for help next time?"

Will this approach work the first time you do it? Of course not! This approach is all about strengthening the synaptic connections that you want to flourish, and encouraging the pruning of synaptic connections that do not serve your child. Fortunately, temper tantrums, picky eating, and other undesired toddler and preschooler behaviors tend to diminish over time, even without intervention.

Neurocognitive Development of School-Age Children and Teenagers

A lot of research has been focused on brain development in children ages five years old and younger. Synaptic connections form during this time at a rate faster than any other time during brain development. But what happens to the brain during the school-age years? It's actually kind of boring, which is probably why information about the brain development of school-age children is harder to find.

From ages six to eleven years old, the brain settles down a bit but development continues. Synaptic connections are being strengthened and those that are not being used are pruned. Different parts of the brain develop at different times, and different parts of the brain develop at different rates. Life experiences continue to be the primary force in shaping this development.

During the school-age years, vocabulary increases. Children develop longer attention spans. Their problem-solving skills increase. They are more independent with self-care activities, such as showering and brushing their teeth. Motor skills continue to develop. School-age kids learn how to ride a bike and how to tie their shoes. They become more proficient at activities that they are interested in, whether that be sports, music, or artistic endeavors.

School age is often a sweet spot during parenting. Picky eating often lessens, temper tantrums become less frequent, and aggressive behaviors such as hitting and biting resolve. School-age children are more independent. They sleep through the night, which has a profound effect on parenting attitudes. Yet, as school-age children get older, they challenge authority. This is normal! In fact, this is just a preview of the years to come.

Of course, school-age children can still demonstrate challenging behaviors. Wanting to be on some type of electronic device for hours on end, refusing to do homework, and not listening are common problematic behaviors of school-age children. Because their frontal lobes are more developed than those of toddlers, you can actually reason with them when they are calm.

Let's go through an example. Your son is in fifth grade. You check his assignment notebook and realize that he did not complete his math homework. After dinner, you ask him why the assignment was not completed. He says, "I don't know." By the way, the phrase "I don't know" is a classic response when a child does not want to get into trouble. More on this phrase later.

Let's get back to the example. In attempts to promote the development of the frontal lobes, you calmly respond, "I noticed that you were playing video games when I got home from work. Do you think it's possible that you didn't do your homework because you were busy playing video games? Maybe we need to create a rule that video games cannot be played until homework is completed. How do you feel about that?"

This may or may not be the reason that your son did not complete his assignment. However, there are a few key points to highlight with this approach. Yelling did not occur. That's parenting win number 1. In addition, you open the door to further reflection and discussion. You encourage your child to think about their actions, as well as the consequences of their actions. That's parenting win number 2. This encourages development of the frontal lobes. Finally, you suggest a behavior that is desired in the future, and you ask your child how they feel about that solution. Those are parenting wins number 3 and 4.

By the way, you are the parent and you are in charge. If failing to complete homework becomes a regular occurrence, consistent consequences need to be implemented.

Eventually school-age children become teenagers, and unfortunately teenagers get a bad rap. They are often considered to be moody, dramatic, self-centered, and defiant. I have cared for many amazing teens over the years, and trust me when I tell you that teenagers are misunderstood.

Here is the neuroscience of the teenage brain. During the teenage years, the brain is still making neural connections between the emotional centers of the brain and the neocortex. The rational, logical, stop-myself-before-I-do-something-stupid part of the part of the brain is not fully developed in teenagers. But whereas younger children are susceptible to amygdala-driven responses, teenagers are more susceptible to having their nucleus accumbens take over.

The nucleus accumbens is a part of the brain that is highly involved with reward and motivation. Just like the amygdala, the nucleus accumbens is a structure within the limbic system, the emotional and reactive part of the forebrain. When a person engages in something that is pleasurable, the nucleus accumbens releases dopamine. This feel-good neurochemical helps us to seek out things that are pleasurable.

From prehistoric times, the nucleus accumbens has been important for helping humans seek out food, sex, and attachment—which are important for survival. In the caveman days, teenagers frequently roamed about, seeking food and mates. While teens no longer need to hunt for food for survival, exploration is still important to help them prepare for adulthood.

Exploration inherently involves the unknown, which also involves risk. Teenagers often get labeled as risk-takers who have little regard for the consequences of their actions. This is not the case. In my experience, teenagers do not engage in risky behaviors simply because of the inherent risk involved. There are much more complicated matters involved.

There is a difference between risk-taking and ambiguity. Risk-taking involves engaging in a behavior that is known to have a potential negative outcome. On the other hand, ambiguity involves being unaware of the potential for negative outcomes. A teenager may engage in a risky behavior simply because they do not completely understand the potential ramifications of their actions. That's why it is so important to have regular discussions with teenagers about the dangers of unprotected sex, drug use, vaping, social media, and bullying.

Adults with fully developed brains learn from both positive and negative outcomes. If an adult engages in a behavior that leads to a positive outcome, they are more likely to repeat that behavior in the future. Likewise, if an adult engages in a behavior that produces a negative outcome, they are more likely to avoid that behavior in the future. The teenage brain is not quite sophisticated enough for this. That's why a teenager may continue to engage in a behavior that has produced a negative outcome in the past.

Time for an example. Let's say that your sixteen-year-old son recently got a ticket for speeding. He had his license for less than a year when he was pulled over. You paid the necessary fine, provided a consequence for his actions, and three weeks later he was ticketed again, for the same reason. While your fully developed brain may have told you to pay attention to the speed limit, your teenager's brain didn't quite get the message.

A major difference between teens and adults is in what is valued. Teenagers will engage in behaviors that stimulate their brain's reward system, based on what they believe to be important. They will gravitate toward actions that make them feel good in the moment, rather on those that will support their long-term goals. You have the nucleus accumbens to thank for this. Again, this is why they are prone to engaging in problematic behavior.

Finally, it is important to understand that a teenager will act based on their personal belief system, and not necessarily on the belief system that their parent wants them to have. As hard as it may be, parents must allow their children to explore their own belief systems. Forcing your beliefs onto your children will backfire. This will result in teenagers who become defiant and rebellious, or meek and subservient. Neither is a desirable outcome.

If you understand what your child's individual values are, you will be more equipped to understand their behaviors. You don't have to agree with those values, and you have a responsibility to provide consequences for behaviors that are unwanted. It's a delicate balance. To make it more complicated, a teenager's values may change over time. Make sure to allow them the opportunity to change their mind, and give them grace as they are trying to figure out who they are and how they fit into the world around them.

The drive to seek pleasurable experiences helps to explain many teenage behaviors which seem irrational to adults. For example, the teen who is engaging in risky sexual behaviors may be seeking approval and acceptance. She may feel insecure, lack a strong male role model, or feel that she needs more attention than she is getting. On the other hand, the teen who engages in activism may value social justice. She may have a strong sense of what it right and what is wrong, and feels compelled to do her part to dispel injustices.

Teenagers are acutely aware of their social world, and the teenage brain is highly rewarded by peer approval. Teenagers are more likely to engage in risk-taking behaviors when their peers are present. For teens, they may choose to engage in a particular behavior because the social benefits outweigh the possible consequences of that behavior. However, that's not to say that teens ignore the behavior of their parents. Teenagers may alter their behavior based upon the risky behavior they observe their parents engage in.

Why do some teens engage in risky behaviors while others are more motivated by altruistic values? The answer is exceedingly complex. Life experiences, personal and family values, peer relationships and ambiguity all play a role. Providing a consistent, safe, and secure home life while allowing the teen to explore new experiences, within reason, will help to encourage navigation of the world around them.

Allowing your teenager to have their own beliefs and values, while simultaneously trying to understand their views, will ultimately strengthen your relationship. This may be challenging, but it is an essential parenting skill. It means that you need to keep your ego in check. I need you to get on board with accepting that it's okay if your teen does not have the same values and beliefs that you do.

Do not force your beliefs on your child. Do not expect your child to view the world in the same manner that you view the world. Listen to your child, and seek to understand their perspective. If you don't, your child will end up resenting you.

This is a challenging task for a lot of parents. It takes a strong, confident person to allow their child to have values and beliefs that are different from their own. Again, a teenager's values and belief systems may change over time. Be flexible and understanding. Your child is a unique individual, and your job is to help them navigate their world, even if that world is not exactly the same as your world.

5

The Theory of Cognitive Development

In the previous chapters, you learned about how the brain is structured and how it develops over time. It's time to understand how children use that magnificent brain to think and to learn about the world around them. In order to do this, I am going to discuss cognitive development, which involves the ways in which kids learn in order to acquire knowledge.

Throughout this book, I am going to introduce you to a few influential psychologists. I find that the theories developed by these psychologists can help people to parent in a more effective, enjoyable way. Are these theories perfect? Of course not! However, they do provide interesting and applicable information.

The first psychologist is Jean Piaget, who created a theory based on four stages of cognitive development.[1] Children at different ages and in different stages of development think differently. If we as parents can understand the ways in which our children think during different stages of their lives, imagine how we can apply that information to our parenting strategies. It's similar to teaching a toddler how to ride a tricycle, teaching a preschooler how to ride a big kid bike with training wheels, and teaching a school-age child how to ride a bike without training wheels. The process is similar, but there are subtle nuances.

I have a few words of caution. When it comes to theories, do not take the information at face value. It's a theory, not a proven fact.

Critics of psychological theories often analyze these theories using very black-or-white thinking. I'd rather you get comfortable in the shades of gray. Acknowledge and utilize whatever resonates with you, and leave the rest. Please also understand that the theories I am going to discuss do not take into account the concept of neurodiversity and may not directly apply to neurodivergent children or to children who have developmental delays.

I find a lot of value in Jean Piaget's theory of cognitive development. But I need to warn you: the following information is intense. It is a lot to process. Again, apply what resonates with you in the here and now, and leave the rest. As your child gets older, you can always come back to this information.

Piaget suggests that children progress through four different stages of learning in order to attain and apply knowledge and skills. Piaget called these stages:

1. Sensorimotor Stage (birth to two years old)
2. Preoperational Stage (two to seven years old)
3. Concrete Operational Stage (seven to eleven years old)
4. Formal Operational Stage (twelve to adult)

Please don't get caught up in the terminology; focus on the concepts. It is important to recognize that children advance through these four stages slowly and often in a nonlinear manner. At times, it may seem like your child is taking two steps forward and three steps backward. That is normal!

Sensorimotor Stage

In Piaget's sensorimotor stage, which occurs from birth to two years old, kids learn through sensory experiences. They utilize the senses that they were born with in order to learn about themselves and the world around them. Taste, smell, touch, sight, and hearing are the focus. Initially, this is the only way that they learn. But as infants develop motor skills such as sitting, grabbing, and standing, they learn to coordinate sensations and physical abilities. They stick things in their mouth and chew on them. As they get older, they self-feed and explore the taste and textures of different foods. They eventually walk around and explore their environment.

They start to realize that objects have certain qualities. They will shake a rattle in order to produce the noise a rattle makes. They may throw a toy on the floor to test cause and effect. Will a parent pick up that toy and give it back to them? Later in the sensorimotor stage, children begin to use symbols such as words and images.

One of the major milestones of the sensorimotor stage is something called object permanence. It tends to develop around nine months of age. This is when a child understands that something still exists even though they cannot see it. Have you ever tried playing peek-a-boo with a four-month-old? I bet it didn't turn out the way you expected. That's because a four-month-old lacks the skill of object permanence. They are likely to cry or simply not react at all when you cover your face. However, for a nine-month-old who possesses the skill of object permanence, peek-a-boo is fascinating and the source of endless fun.

How can we apply this to real-life parenting? By focusing on our child's sensory experiences. Smile at your infant and make silly faces. Once they are old enough, play peek-a-boo. Provide them access to toys that they can pick up and play with. Child-proof your home in order for them to explore their environment. Talk about different sensations. Gently splash the water in the tub during their bath and comment on its warmth. When they are eating lunch, talk about how sweet the food tastes.

I strongly recommend that you encourage your sensorimotor child's speech development, because speech is a symbol of thought that we can hear. We do this by reading to our children, and by singing or talking to them even when we are doing mundane tasks such as changing their diaper. In fact, reading to a child for twenty minutes a day can create a profound and lasting impact on a child's development. Research has demonstrated increased vocabulary, increased critical-thinking skills, increased parent-child bond, and assists in the development of empathy.

Quick summary: children from birth to age two learn about the world around them through their senses of sight, hearing, taste, touch, and smell. Identify and discuss those senses verbally and your child will thrive. Don't forget to read to your child—aim for twenty minutes a day.

Preoperational Stage

The preoperational stage is next and encompasses children aged two to seven years old. Imagination is the key feature of this stage. Kids learn through using symbols and by pretending. They may pretend that a plastic baseball bat is actually a horse and ride it around the house. During this stage, children may assign human characteristics to inanimate objects, such as a teddy bear. They often enjoy taking on the roles of others, such as pretending to be a fireman or a superhero.

A hallmark of this stage is something called egocentrism, which involves a child not being able to take on the viewpoint of others. They are only able to experience the world through their own eyes and are unable to understand the perspective of other people. This is often a challenging concept for parents to understand. Due to egocentrism, children at this age may appear to lack empathy.

This is why a child may not seem sad if their friend loses a beloved toy. Or why they do not seem concerned if their sibling has a fever—after all, they are not the one who is sick! It's important to understand that seeing the world through someone else's perspective is a skill that needs to be learned. As a child progresses through the preoperational stage, their degree of egocentrism decreases.

Egocentrism is the reason that children in the preoperational stage often engage in magical thinking. Magical thinking is when someone believes that their thoughts directly influence the world around them and may create a cause-and-effect phenomenon that does not actually exist. For example, a child may believe that they caused their parents to get a divorce because they were "bad" or that their brother broke their arm because the child called him a "poo-poo head."

By the way, magical thinking is not limited to children. Have you ever knocked on wood? Or worn a pair of lucky socks to a job interview? Have you ever told your child to make a wish when they blew out their birthday candles? These are all examples of magical thinking. Magical thinking is not necessarily a bad thing, as long as it does not negatively impact our health or well-being.

How do we apply the preoperational stage to real-life parenting? We embrace the imagination and creativity, and understand that it is a normal part of child development. If our child decides that they are Superman, we buy them a cape. If they determine that they have an imaginary friend who happens to be a unicorn, we ask about the unicorn's name and welcome them into our home. We allow our children to believe in Santa Claus, the Tooth Fairy, and the Easter Bunny.

We also acknowledge and embrace the egocentrism. We don't freak out when our child pushes their friend for stealing a toy that they were playing with. We don't demand our child to explain why they hurt their friend, because we understand that their developing brain is not sophisticated enough to form a response.

It's important to work within the framework of egocentrism instead of fighting against it. Children in the preoperational stage will assign blame to themselves for something that is not their fault, because of the way in which they view the world around them. We need to pay attention to these incorrect cause and effect relationships that preoperational children create.

For example, in the case of divorce, it is very important to explain to the child that they had nothing to do with their parents deciding to go their separate ways. If a sibling breaks an arm, it is important to explain that the injury did not occur because the preoperational child called their sibling a poo-poo head earlier that day. These events may need to be revisited and re-explained as children become less egocentric.

This stage is challenging for many parents because it involves balance! While it's important to encourage and support a child's imagination, it is equally important to gently try to change any such relationship or thought pattern that impairs a child's well-being. This takes practice and a lot of patience, both with your child and with yourself.

Despite the challenges of parenting a preoperational child, I always encourage people to have fun during this stage of their child's development! Pretend that your child's favorite stuffed animal is actually alive. Allow them to wear a baseball helmet everywhere they go. Play kitchen, or school, or pretend dinosaurs with your child. Talk to your child about the point of view of others, even if they don't fully grasp the concept.

Quick summary: Kids in the preoperational stage (aged two through seven years old) learn about the world around them almost exclusively through their own perspective. Encourage imagination. Don't stress out about egocentrism. Acknowledge it, and, at the same time, introduce the view of others into your child's life.

For example, if you are driving your child home from daycare, discuss the temperature in the car. If you feel too warm, verbally acknowledge it and tell your child that you are going to turn down the car's thermostat. For older preoperational kids, ask them how they would respond if someone else engaged in a problematic behavior. If a preoperational child is running around the house yelling "Barbies are stupid!", calmly ask them how they would feel if someone else said that about their favorite toy.

Concrete Operational Stage

Next up is the concrete operational stage, which involves seven- to eleven-year-olds. In this stage, children start to apply logical thought. They begin to analyze a situation and use reasoning to identify ideas or solutions. They apply rules to physical objects. Clear as mud, right?

Let's break it down. Children in this stage think concretely, meaning that they take things literally and base their thinking on what they perceive to be real and tangible.

If you tell a concrete operational thinker that they will break their mother's back if they step on a crack in the sidewalk, they will likely hop over those cracks for fear of hurting their mom. As an adult with a fully developed brain, I understand that this may seem incredulous. Yet it is very real for a child in the concrete operational stage. Let me give you another example.

I love thunderstorms. One day when my daughter was seven years old, we were at home and a massive storm system developed. I opened our front door to watch the rain and said, "It's raining cats and dogs!" My daughter, who is a huge animal lover, tried to run out the door in order to save the kitties and puppies that she assumed were falling from the sky. Luckily, I caught her before she got soaked, and once her tears had stopped, I explained that phrase to her—and promised that I would never use it again.

Children in the concrete operational stage focus on the facts and information available to them in the immediate present. They are able to use logic if it is related to something that they directly observe or experience. They generally understand that individuals possess their own ideas, beliefs, and emotions but are still learning how to adopt the perspectives of others.

Children in this stage are starting to use observations in order to create theories and conclusions. This is called inductive reasoning. For example, they may notice that you sneeze and develop itchy, watery eyes every time you are around cats. Your concrete operational thinker determines that you must be allergic to cats, without you directly telling them that you are allergic to cats.

It's important to note that the theories and conclusions that concrete operational thinkers develop may not be true. For example, if you, your child, and all of their aunts, uncles, and cousins get together to watch Sunday Night Football every weekend, your child may incorrectly assume that everyone enjoys watching Sunday Night Football.

In addition, children in the concrete operational stage are becoming less egocentric. They start to think about the ways in which other people view and experience the world. They begin to use this information to solve problems and make decisions. For example, when two concrete operational thinkers are paired to work together on an assignment about an animal, they have to collaborate and compromise in order to choose a single animal, even if they each have a different favorite animal. This is the exact scenario that happened when my daughter was in second grade. I was surprised to see her book report was about Tasmanian devils. Yet, her friend chose the animal and she was willing to go along.

Finally, children in this stage also develop an understanding of the concepts of reversibility and conservation. Reversibility involves understanding that an object or a number can be changed and then returned to its original condition. Concrete operational thinkers no longer cry that a deflated basketball is broken, because they understand it can be filled with air and return to its original shape. This is an example of reversibility. Conservation involves understanding that an object retains its original volume, mass, or amount when that object changes its form. You can break a candy bar into two pieces, and your child will not think that they are getting less candy because suddenly the pieces are smaller—this is an example of conservation.

Is this starting to seem overwhelming? I get it. Take your time and read the above information over again. My suggestion is to focus on the stage that your child is in and come back to this chapter as your child grows up. There is no need to memorize any of this information. It is here for reference.

Let's summarize. Children aged seven to eleven are considered to be concrete operational thinkers. Direct observations are central to their experience with the world around them. They create theories based on their observations, even if these observations result in incorrect associations. Children in the concrete operational stage think literally, which is why they struggle when someone uses idioms such as "It's raining cats and dogs" or "Break a leg!" They are increasingly more empathetic and more proficient at understanding and accepting that other people have their own thoughts and feelings. They understand that objects can change their form yet retain or regain their original properties.

How do we apply concrete operational learning to real-life parenting? We pay attention to our child's inductive reasoning. Remember, inductive reasoning involves using observation in order to develop broad generalizations. We engage in frequent conversations with our child about their reasoning. We ask them how to came to the conclusion about a generalization that they developed, in a way that demonstrates we are actually interested and are listening to their response.

We may gently need to challenge the truth or accuracy of the generalizations, but we simultaneously validate the thought process that led to those conclusions. As parents, we explain any untrue generalizations in a nonjudgmental manner.

Here's an example. Let's say that your family has a black Labrador retriever as a pet, as does the neighbor down the street. Both dogs bark loudly. Your concrete operational thinker incorrectly assumes that all black dogs bark loudly. In order to encourage neurocognitive development, it would be beneficial to introduce that child to other dogs of different colors who also bark loudly or to a black dog that doesn't bark very much. Doing so without judgment or dismissal of the previously made generalization will encourage cognitive development.

For a concrete operational thinker who is learning the essential skill of conflict resolution, consider the following. If your child is involved in a conflict with another child, it's important to discuss the incident from both your child's perspective (in order to validate your child's experience) and from the other child's perspective (in order to validate the other child's experience). We ask our child, "How do you think that made them feel?" Again, ask in an instructional and nonjudgmental manner. Parenting is about instruction, not asserting power.

Formal Operational Stage

Piaget's final stage of cognitive development is the formal operational stage, which occurs from twelve years old to adulthood. The hallmark features of this stage are abstraction, deductive logic, and organized problem-solving skills. The ability to think abstractly involves understanding that certain concepts are real, even if they are not directly related to physical objects or experiences. Abstraction is about ideas rather than physical objects or events. Dad jokes, the concept of success, and freedom are all examples of abstraction.

Deductive logic involves using principles believed to be true in order to create theories or conclusions. An example involves a child who is told that they have outgrown their current shoes and that they need to put on new shoes. The new shoes fit well. Therefore, the child understands that the old shoes are in fact too small, without directly being told that their old shoes are too small. Here's another example of deductive reasoning: all fruits have seeds. A strawberry is a fruit. Therefore, strawberries have seeds.

Problem-solving is the process of identifying, analyzing, and solving problems. This is actually more complex than it seems. Successfully identifying a problem involves correctly determining the source of the problem. Analyzing the problem involves assessing the available information, breaking the problem down into components, and setting goals for addressing those components. Finally, solving problems depends on identifying strategies to solve the problem and allocating appropriate resources to do so.

Here's an example. Let's say that you are the parent of fourteen-year-old Sean. Sean loves to play tennis but is struggling with his backhand. He is so frustrated that he is contemplating not trying out for his high school's tennis team. He assumes that he won't make the team and doesn't want to embarrass himself.

Time to help Sean break it down. The problem is his backhand. Yet, it's important to get more specific. Is the problem in his technique? Is he using the best racket for his age and skill set? Does he just need more practice? Fortunately, Sean has a tennis coach who can help him work through this problem. He decides to record Sean hitting a backhand, in order to be able to view his backhand in slow motion. When Sean and his coach review the video, they determine together that Sean struggles to get into the correct position quickly enough, and his grip could improve. Sean's coach recommends practicing on a clay court, because the surface of the court slows down the play of the game. Sean is on board, and within a few months, his backhand has improved dramatically. Problem solved.

Are your eyes glazed over? Again, I get it. This is high-level stuff. Again, the information is presented for completeness. I'll be honest. I never think about my children's behavior in terms of their deductive reasoning skills. I don't sit around and ponder their ability to think abstractly. Yet, I utilize these concepts in order to shape my parenting strategies.

How do we apply the formal operational stage to real-life parenting? We encourage the processes involved in problem-solving, even if the problem is never actually solved. We discuss abstract concepts with our children, such as humor, love, and friendships, on a regular basis. We encourage them to use their theories to create conclusions, then ask them if those conclusions are actually true.

Children in the formal operational stage are able to plan an organized approach to solving a problem. A child in the concrete operational stage will rely on trial and error to solve a problem. Children in the formal operational stage are able to think about their own thoughts. A child in the concrete operational stage is still learning to get past egocentrism.

If your brain is spinning in attempts to try to wrap your brain around these concepts, I get it. I want to make sure that I am thorough in the explanation of Piaget's work. Yet, I understand how dry some of this material may be. As I have mentioned several times, they are here as a reference. Come back to the explanations as often as you need to. Use the information that is helpful in parenting your unique child. Theory is not fact. In fact, several modern-day psychologists have challenged some of Piaget's ideas and have very valid points.

The take-away messages are these:

Jean Piaget was a psychologist who developed a theory about how children acquire knowledge and apply information. From birth to two years old, children primarily learn about the world through their senses—sight, sound, smell, touch, and taste. As they progress through the sensorimotor stage, they begin to coordinate senses with physical abilities. From two to seven years old, children typically lack the ability to view the world through anyone else's perspective, though this is a skill that is developing. Initially, they assume that everyone sees and experiences the world in the same way that they do. They use imagination and pretend to explore their world.

From seven to eleven years old, children are very literal. They create conclusions based on personal observations. These conclusions may or may not be true. They are starting to understand the perspectives of others but are not yet proficient at utilizing this skill in social situations. Finally, children aged twelve and older are able to think abstractly, meaning that they understand certain concepts are real, even if there is no physical object or experience attached to that concept. They make specific inferences based on general laws. By no means does that mean that a twelve-year-old has the same cognitive skills as a grown adult.

Why does this complicated information even matter? Because it can help you understand the child that you have. Let me give you an example. Many years ago, I had a patient schedule an appointment for a behavioral evaluation for their three-year-old child. The family was distraught that this child was hurting other people and did not seem sad about it. Let's call this child Emma.

In one instance, Emma pushed child A when he stole a toy that her imaginary friend Emmett was playing with. Child A proceeded to fall down and cry. In another instance, Emma witnessed child B fall off of the swing next to her swing and did not cry when that child seemed to be hurt. The daycare expressed concern about Emma's lack of empathy.

When I questioned the family about Emma's behavior at home, her grandmother was very concerned that Emma hit others. I asked her, "What do you do when she hits?" The grandmother looked at me like I had three heads and said, "I ask her why she hit me of course!"

In the scenario with child A, Emma felt threatened. Her imaginary friend is very real to her, and the imaginary friend's turf was invaded. As a result, her amygdala lit up, and the fight-flight-freeze response kicked in. She wasn't intentionally trying to hurt child A; she was reacting to a perceived threat.

In the scenario with child B, this was all about egocentrism. Emma was not the one who fell off of the swing and got hurt. At her age, she does not understand the perspective of others and should not be expected to do so. Emma assumes that her own internal states and emotions are the same as those around her, which is developmentally appropriate at this age.

Finally, in the grandmother's scenario, yikes! Talk about unrealistic expectations. Remember, a three-year-old has little to no ability to be rational. They cannot think about their behavior, understand why it was problematic, and explain that behavior to others. In Emma's case, understanding and setting developmentally appropriate expectations would have helped everyone involved.

Fast forward a few years, and now Emma is seven years old. She is struggling a bit in school. At parent-teacher conferences, Emma's teacher had a few concerns. She reported that on several occasions, Emma disrupted the classroom by "scooting on her butt" to move to a new location she was not asked to move to. She became very upset and yelled at a child who told her that he had seen a pink duck, because pink ducks don't exist. When a teacher's aide told the class that she celebrated Hanukkah and explained the significance of this event, Emma became upset because Santa Claus was not involved in everyone's holiday celebrations.

Emma's behaviors were actually very much appropriate based on her cognitive development. After a brief discussion, it was determined that Emma was asked to "scoot over" when she sat too close to another student. She took this literally, sat on her butt, and scooted across the room. In addition, she thinks concretely and knows that pink ducks are not real. She took the boy's comment as lying, which she learned was wrong because of the rules her family has. Finally, she created an incorrect cause and effect relationship between winter holidays and Santa Claus because Emma and her family celebrate Christmas.

Piaget's theory of cognitive development can help parents set appropriate expectations for behavior while simultaneously helping their child to develop cognitive abilities. Again, children with developmental delays or who are neurodivergent may not progress through these stages as Piaget proposed. That is okay! Work with the child that you have, and do not get caught up in the age-specific information. Use the information that benefits you and your child when it comes to their cognitive development.

PART II

EMOTIONAL DEVELOPMENT

6

Understanding Emotions and the Dangers of Emotional Suppression

Many adults suck at managing emotions. It's not our fault, because the things that we have been taught about emotions and feelings have been unpleasant or downright untrue. How many times in your life have you been told:

- You're not (insert emotion here)
- Stop crying!
- Grow up and be a man!
- Don't act like such a baby!

We have been led to believe that emotions make us "weak." That we need to "pull up our bootstraps" and get over it. We are taught to ignore or suppress our emotions. Don't believe me? Think about this: When someone asks, "How are you?" how do you respond? I bet you say "I'm good" even if you aren't. You may be insanely happy or in the depths of grief, yet you won't admit to it. Unfortunately, the expression of emotions has long been considered socially unacceptable.

Yet emotions are fundamental in our experience as human beings. If you grew up in a family that did not value emotions, get ready for a challenge. The only way out is through. You need to allow yourself to feel your feelings, learn how to express those feelings in a healthy and appropriate manner, and do so without judging yourself. Then you need to teach your children how to do the exact same thing. This is much easier said than done. Be patient with yourself and keep trying. Every emotion that you experience is a chance for you to gain a deeper understanding.

I use the terms "emotions" and "feelings" interchangeably. They are slightly different. To me, emotions are experienced in the brain and feelings are experienced in the body. For example, when someone experiences anger, they may think about how mad they are. This is the emotion of anger. Yet often simultaneously, they feel a burning sensation or a tightness in their chest. Their heart may beat faster and their hands may clench. This is the feeling of anger. For most people who are uncomfortable with these concepts, it may be impossible to differentiate between feelings and emotions, at least initially. That's okay!

From an evolutionary standpoint, emotions were essential for survival. If we never felt fear, we wouldn't run away from saber-toothed tigers who were trying to eat us. If we never felt love, we would not care for our offspring and instead would abandon them in the woods. Emotions are a normal, natural part of our existence as human beings.

No emotion is inherently bad or wrong. Let this sink in. Every single emotion that we experience is valid and important. Anger, sadness, guilt, shame, disgust, and annoyance are considered negative emotions, meaning that they are emotions most people don't want to experience. They are uncomfortable, but they are an essential part of our experience as human beings. It's time to get comfortable with the uncomfortable.

I once had a teenage patient who was struggling with major depressive disorder. When I was speaking with her and her dad about treatment options, the dad looked at me and said, "My people don't take pills for depression. We drink and do drugs." Sadly, the look on his face told me that he wasn't kidding. Yet, the simple fact that this man brought his daughter to see me told me that he was open to change. Unfortunately, many people develop unhealthy and potentially dangerous habits in order to cope with difficult emotions.

People who experience negative emotions may look toward alcohol, food, or drugs to numb out. Unfortunately, these methods are fleeting. When the high wears off, when the hangover kicks in, those emotions are present and may be felt even stronger. If you are in this group, please don't feel bad. Many of us have not been taught how to experience emotions in a healthy manner.

Please understand that there is no judgment here. I used to drink alcohol excessively in an attempt to numb my emotions. Prior to my alcohol use, I was an emotional eater. My emotional eating morphed into a very serious eating disorder that almost cost me my career. At the heart of my issues was a difficulty in understanding and expressing my emotions.

I grew up in a home where emotional expression was not welcomed. Like many others, it was only acceptable for me to be "fine" or "good" or "okay." Anything else, such as being sad, angry, or even happy, was considered rude or unlikable. As a result, I feared emotions and suppressed them at all costs. It took me decades of therapy to learn how to feel, acknowledge, and express my emotions in a healthy manner.

In order to be exceptional parents, we need to understand our emotions and get used to feeling them. We then need to learn how to express those emotions in a healthy manner in order to let them go. Again, this may be easier said than done!

The challenge here is twofold. First, you must accept that emotions are essential to our experience as human beings and embrace the concept that no emotions are inherently good or bad. You need to accept that emotions are important and valid, and not inherently problematic. You have to feel what you feel without judging yourself. Second, you must recognize that there are healthy and unhealthy ways to cope with emotions, and that as a parent, you have a responsibility to express your emotions in a healthy manner.

Emotional expression involves verbal and nonverbal behaviors that communicate your emotional state to the world. If your child observes you punch a hole in a wall because you are angry, they will learn that this is an appropriate way to deal with anger. On the other hand, if you feel angry, express this emotion to your child, then run a mile to help you let that anger go, your child will learn that this is an appropriate way to deal with anger. Similarly, if they see you eat a gallon of ice cream when you are sad, your child will learn to become an emotional eater. If they see you cry when you are sad, your child will learn that crying is an appropriate way to deal with sadness. The reason for this is called modeling, which will be discussed soon.

It's important to focus on the trend over time. We all lose our cool and act in a manner that we regret from time to time. Yet if you are able to express your emotions in a healthy manner at least 85 percent of the time, congratulations. I encourage you to create that as a benchmark.

For those who are struggling to meet that benchmark, be patient with yourself. If you feel uncomfortable with experiencing and expressing emotions, take it one emotion at a time. Allow yourself to experience your emotions and feelings without judging them and without judging yourself for experiencing that emotion. Make sure to notice how that emotion feels in your body.

No feelings are final. I learned this from my amazing therapist, Heather. Whenever you are faced with an emotion, don't try to dissipate it. Acknowledge it. If you can, allow that emotion to come into your conscious awareness, no matter how uncomfortable or unpleasant it may be. Take a few slow, deep breaths and allow yourself to experience the emotion. Welcome it. Learn from it. Know that the emotion will pass. And when it does, please congratulate yourself.

When I first started to acknowledge my emotions, sometimes I didn't even know what to call them. It's actually more important to describe the emotion rather than to label it. For example, over time I came to realize that I feel sadness in my chest. It feels cold and wet. I feel anxiety in my jaw, posterior neck, chest, and upper back. It feels warm and uncomfortably tight. I feel anger in my gut. It feels like a gnawing, sharp pain.

You don't have to name an emotion in order to experience it and let it pass. You just need to allow the emotion to come to the surface and feel it. Allow the emotion into your conscious experience. Experience it in its fullness. Deal with it in a healthy manner. Not sure if your expression of emotions is healthy?

Here are a few examples of healthy emotional expression:

- Journaling
- Drawing, coloring, or painting
- Exercise
- Mindfulness
- Punching a pillow
- Talking to a loved one
- Screaming into a pillow

Emotions can temporarily be pushed out of our conscious awareness, but they don't go away until they are resolved. Unresolved emotions will fester, get stronger, and eventually bubble up to conscious awareness, usually in a dramatic fashion. The good news is that simply allowing yourself to feel the feeling without judgment will often lead to resolution. However, for many of us, this is easier said than done. Rather than encouraging healthy emotional expression, we often turn to unhealthy methods that keep the true emotions under the surface, just waiting to explode.

Ignoring our emotions, trying to eat or drink them away, doing drugs, road rage, and screaming at our loved ones are unhealthy examples of expressing our emotions. If you have ever used any of these methods to try to cope with your emotions, that's okay! You are definitely not alone. You did the best that you could at the time, and now it is time to learn to do better. You and your kids deserve it.

The only way to determine which healthy outlet for emotions works best for you is to try them. It's trial and error, and please have grace for yourself during this process. It took me a long time, but eventually, I learned that I manage my anger best by doing a mixed martial arts workout. I manage loneliness best by journaling. I manage sadness and grief best by crying. Are there times that I drink a few glasses of wine because I'm sad about something that happened to one of my patients? Yep. I'm human, and I'm doing the best that I can.

It's not always feasible to engage in our preferred healthy outlets exactly when we need them. It's not like I'm going to start boxing while I'm at work! Sometimes, we need to save the emotional expression for a later time. Delaying our emotional expression until it is situationally appropriate benefits both parents and children. For example, if your boss made negative comments about your job performance in front of the entire office, it's normal to feel angry. Instead of screaming at your boss, you wait until you are home and then scream into a pillow. Congratulations. You have expressed an emotion in a healthful manner.

If you are still feeling the emotion after you attempted a healthy expression, gently ask yourself why. Are you angry or sad about something else? What else is going on in your emotional world? What do you need? Please be kind and do not judge yourself, because this will interfere with your ability to fully understand your experience.

In my home, we don't shy away from the tough stuff. If we are sad, or happy, or anxious, we don't hide those feelings. My husband and I allow our children to witness our behavioral responses to our emotions. We have discussions about the expression of emotions when it is needed. As a pediatrician, one of the most difficult emotional experiences that I face is when one of my patients dies. It's rare for my patients to pass away, but when they do, it's gut-wrenching.

A young infant in my medical practice died, presumably from sudden infant death syndrome (SIDS), because she had been co-sleeping with other people. I was not only the pediatrician to this infant; I had been the pediatrician to her mom before she grew up and had kids of her own. This infant's death was completely preventable, and it brought up a lot of emotions for me. When I found out about the incident, anger, grief, disbelief, and sadness all bubbled to the surface.

As soon as I got home, I briefly told my husband what had happened. He also appreciates the importance of emotional expression and told me to take all the time that I needed. I went into our basement gym, did a mixed martial arts workout, and let myself feel it all. At the end of the workout, I let out a scream and fell to the floor sobbing. I cried so hard that my kids could hear me. After a few minutes, I felt better. I took a shower then sat my kids down at the kitchen table to explain why mommy had shouted and cried, in developmentally appropriate terms.

Emotions are essential to our experience as human beings. Rather than shying away from these emotions, we need to understand them, accept them, and embrace them. If we don't, we are doing our children a disservice.

When I was eleven years old, my paternal grandmother died from endometrial cancer. I was absolutely devastated. My grandmother was the one person in my life who loved me unconditionally. I felt warm and safe around her. She used to let me sit on her lap while she brushed my hair, and each time she did so, I felt important and special.

My grandmother's death was traumatic for me in so many ways. I was in her home when she died. I vividly remember my mom giving her a sponge bath in her bed only hours before her passing. Her fancy perfume bottles were on her dresser, and a scary picture of Jesus bleeding from a crown of thorns was hanging on the wall above her head. She was severely bloated from the cancer and not completely conscious due to the pain medication that kept her minimally comfortable.

I don't remember the exact moment that she died. But I do remember the aftermath. Paramedics arrived at her home. My dad told me to cover my eyes, but I watched as the paramedics wheeled a cart with a white sheet over my grandmother's dead body out of her home.

It was late at night, and I was really tired. Nobody talked much. The days that followed were simultaneously insanely long and incredibly short. The adults intentionally pushed the children away. There were a lot of hushed conversations. A few days later, it was time for the funeral.

I remember the details vividly. I wore a sunflower dress from The Limited Too to my grandmother's funeral. Her casket was a beautiful shade of medium blue. The funeral home smelled strongly of flowers. Lots of people tried to hug me, which made me uncomfortable. As I looked at my grandmother for the last time, I was convinced that I could see her breathing. I wanted to jump into the casket and squeeze her as hard as I could.

My immediate family rode in a black limousine to the cemetery. A large bouquet of white roses was placed on the casket before my grandmother's dead body was lowered into the ground. Nobody said anything. After the funeral, we went to a Polish restaurant for lunch. After that, everyone went home and that was that.

The adults had significant conflicts over my grandmother's will, of which my dad was the executor and thus in charge. They kept the details of those conflicts away from the kids, though I later learned that the source of the conflict was a pool table. Yet because of that conflict, my aunt, uncle, and two cousins no longer associated with my immediate family. Neither did my great aunt or my second cousins. Talk about grief compounded. I not only lost my grandmother; I lost the rest of my extended paternal family as well.

No one talked to me or my brother about grief. Everyone just went on with their lives. As a result, I became a people-pleaser. My extended family stopped liking my dad, so I assumed they didn't like me either. My little kid rationale at the time was that if people liked me, they wouldn't leave me. I became terrified of disappointing others and having people leave me. As a result, I became a people-pleaser. Cue the concrete operational inductive reasoning. After my grandmother's death, I started emotionally eating. I would come home from school, dump two scoops of vanilla ice cream into a cup, then pour a can of Pepsi over it. I drank two Pepsi floats per day, all before dinner.

I firmly believe that the lack of communication and the lack of acknowledgment were my parents' ways of trying to "shield" me and my brother from the trauma related to my grandmother's death. I believe that their intention was good. Unfortunately, it did the exact opposite of the intent. The attempts to shield me from pain did nothing other than contribute to isolation, emotional suppression, and the development of unhealthy coping mechanisms.

We all experience trauma, whether that be in the form of a loved one's death, divorce, loss of income, or significant illness. Whoever experiences the trauma needs support. They need to be encouraged to express their emotions. Those emotions need to be validated and not dismissed. At the same time, those emotions need to be expressed and not "bought" away with gifts.

I have a patient in my medical practice whose father passed away after an accidental overdose on heroin that was laced with fentanyl. She was very young at the time of his passing. The father's family's response to her trauma was to buy her lots of toys. The mother was distraught, because her daughter was acting out, throwing and breaking most of those toys. This child did not need "stuff"; she needed help navigating the difficult situation surrounding her father's death.

Be honest about your emotions, both to yourself and to your children. Kids are smart, and they are able to pick up on subtle emotional cues. If you are angry, stomping around the house, and slamming doors, please do not tell your children that you are fine. They know that you are not fine, and telling them that you are fine undercuts their own emotional development.

Your children learn how to experience and regulate their own emotions by watching you experience and regulate your own emotions. That is a lot of responsibility. However, being accepting of your positive and negative emotions helps your children to become accepting of their own emotions.

Talk about your emotions in front of your child. Explain why you are feeling that way in developmentally appropriate terms. Allow your child to watch you process that emotion in a healthy manner and eventually let that emotion go. Even if your child is in Piaget's sensorimotor or preoperational stage, discussing your emotions helps their brain development. They may not be able to understand your perspective, but it still encourages the development of synaptic connections.

Never tell your child that they are "making" you feel a certain way. Why? Because no one can make another person feel anything. Emotions are a personal experience, created in our own psyche. Did your mom ever tell you, "You embarrassed me!" or "See how sad I am? You made my heart hurt." Yep, me too. It's time to break the cycle.

You are the only one who is in charge of your emotions. You are the only one who is in charge of the actions that are the result of your emotions. Likewise, your child is the only one in charge of their emotions. Can our thoughts and behaviors influence our emotions? Of course! But that again involves no one but ourselves.

No one can create an emotional experience within another person. As a parent, it is important to watch what you say. Instead of saying, "You make me so mad!", consider saying, "I feel mad when I see you throw your crayons. Can you please ask for my help instead?" The latter not only individualizes the emotional experience, it also offers a future solution to the undesirable behavior. That's a win-win for everyone involved.

Sometimes, parents don't want to admit to experiencing negative emotions. Have you ever heard someone say, "Not in front of the kids?" The intention behind this statement is usually positive. Yet attempting to shield a child from painful experiences and/or negative emotions does more harm than good. Please do not try to hide negative emotions or painful experiences from your children. This will backfire.

I know that you want to protect your little loves. Unfortunately, the world we live in is, at times, full of pain and strife and challenges. Shielding your child from these struggles impairs their growth. When you experience any emotion, the best course of action is to let your children see how you work through it. It's important to be authentic in the expression of emotions. In fact, doing so helps to build resilience.

If we are angry, we should let our kids know why we are angry. Again, we want to be age-appropriate and developmentally appropriate in our response. If you are angry because you just found out that your best friend's husband is a no-good, cheating liar, you may want to keep that information to yourself. However, it would be perfectly fine to tell your five-year-old that you are angry because Brian is a big meanie and you no longer want to be friends with him.

Don't be afraid to cry in front of your child, even if it initially seems to cause them some distress. We need to help our children learn how to work through that distress. Both of my kids become upset when they see me cry. Yet I cry in front of them anyways. Not only do I want to normalize crying when someone is sad, but I want them to see how much better I feel after I can release the emotion of sadness.

Emotions don't have to be scary or uncomfortable. In fact, every single time that your child watches you experience an emotion, they learn how to deal with their own emotions. When your child expresses their own emotion in a positive manner, please praise them and ask them if they need anything from you.

Within your home, try to create an environment that encourages emotional expression. Be accepting of all emotions, and be willing to have open and honest discussions about emotions, even if those emotions are perceived to be negative. It benefits your kids to observe how you experience, express, and release your emotions. Pay attention to the verbal and nonverbal manners in which you express your emotions, and remember that no feeling is final. Don't be afraid to talk about your experiences; just do your best to be age and developmentally appropriate in those discussions.

7

The Relationship between Thoughts, Emotions, and Behavior

Thoughts, emotions, and behaviors are intimately related. I like to think of them as three sides of a triangle, with a double-sided arrow between each side. This is called the cognitive behavior therapy (CBT) triangle. This is the basis of something called CBT, developed in the 1960s by Aaron Beck and Albert Ellis. The CBT triangle suggests that if you change one point in the triangle, you can also change the other two points. Much of the time, the relationship between thoughts, emotions, and actions are unconscious. Yet making an attempt to bring them into conscious awareness can have profound effects.

Let's go through an example. Your two-year-old is sick with a bad cold. She was awake all night coughing, which means that you did not get much sleep. You are insanely tired. You are frustrated because there is nothing that you can do to make your child better; it's a viral illness and there are no medications to make it go away faster. She is cranky, and so are you. The next morning, you are trying to get the older kids ready for school. Your five-year-old accidentally spills an entire cup of water and you go ballistic. You lose your cool and scream about the mess.

When an adult has an intense emotional reaction that is out of proportion to the circumstance that triggered the reaction, this is called "amygdala hijack." This term was explored in detail by Daniel Goleman in his book *Emotional Intelligence: Why It Can Matter More than IQ*.[1] When adults experience strong emotions and are unable to use their prefrontal cortex to modulate their behavioral response, amygdala hijack occurs.

The parent's response to the above scenario is the result of an amygdala hijack. The adult brain perceived a threat (spilled water) and reacted with a fight mentality (screaming at the child who created the threat). Amygdala hijack can cause grown adults to say or do things that they don't mean, because their frontal lobes have been bypassed. The primitive brain takes over, rational thought goes out the window, and emotions drive the behavior.

Let's go through another example. This one is an example of using the frontal lobes to improve behavior. A few years ago, I was burnt out; working full time as a pediatrician and raising two young strong-willed kids left me exhausted. I was taking care of others, at my own expense, for years. This caused me to feel resentment. I was frequently cranky and was regularly drinking alcohol every evening in an attempt to deal with the stress. I decided, with the support of my husband, that instead of grabbing a bottle of wine, I would go to our basement to exercise as soon as I got home from work.

Initially, I felt insanely guilty. I was taking an hour a day, three days a week, to take care of myself. If my children needed something during that time, my husband would step up and provide for them. In all honesty, I felt like a bad mom. But at the same time, I knew that my current behavior was not good for me, my husband, or my children.

After a few weeks, I noticed something incredible. I was calmer. I was more present with my children and with my husband during the time we spent together. I was happier. My kids and my husband sensed this shift, and they welcomed it. Sometimes, my kids would join me during my workouts, which was awesome. I first changed my behavior, which led to changes in my emotions and thoughts.

I encourage you to become aware of your thoughts, emotions, and actions, and not from a punitive, guilt-ridden, or shaming perspective. Once you become aware, you can understand. Once you understand, you can change thoughts and behaviors that do not serve you.

If that sounds too good to be true, it's not. It just takes a hell of a lot of work. The first step is to become aware of your thoughts. Why? Because when it comes to the CBT triangle, the most common scenario is that thoughts lead to emotions, and emotions lead to behavior. Can emotions lead to thoughts? Of course! Can behaviors lead to thoughts? Sure thing. But the most common sequence is that thoughts lead to emotions, and emotions lead to behavior.

I have an exercise for you to complete. I want you to carry a notebook around and write down every single thought you have for an entire day. Every single thought? Yes, every single thought. No thought is too insignificant to write down. Do this for one day then put that notebook down.

I am completely serious about this. If you want to become aware of your thoughts, you need to complete this exercise. I understand how time-consuming and mentally draining this exercise can be. I've done it myself on numerous occasions. Yet this is a very effective method to become aware of your thoughts, which most of the time exist below the level of our conscious awareness. If you miss a few thoughts, that's okay! It's not about perfection; it's about the process.

I know what you are thinking. How does making notes of my thoughts make me a better parent? Most of us have recurrent thoughts that we are usually unaware of. Bringing those thoughts into conscious awareness is important. The best way to do this is to become aware and write them down. The time you invest in writing your thoughts down will pay off in dividends.

Once you have recorded your thoughts without judgment, I want you to put those notes away for a few days. Give your brain a bit of a break. And don't forget to give yourself credit for doing something that was previously out of your comfort zone.

After a few days, I want you to open those notes. I want you to analyze them. I want you to ask yourself a few questions. Are there thoughts that seem to repeat themselves throughout your day? Most of us have a few thoughts that are on autopilot. Examples include, "I'm so fat!" or "I'm a bad mom" or "I suck at this!"

Make a note of three to five repetitive phrases, then move on to the next step of this exercise, which involves the analysis of the repetitive thoughts. Slowly and intentionally analyze those thoughts one by one. For each thought, complete the following process:

1. Is that thought actually your own? Determine if you alone created that thought or if someone else planted that thought in your brain. You'd be surprised at how many of your thoughts are not your own.

2. Is that thought actually true? Not all of our thoughts are.

3. Is that thought serving you? Does that thought make you feel good and create positive emotions or behaviors? If so, it is serving you. If the thought makes you feel like crap, it is not serving you.

The third and final step of this exercise is to change the thoughts that are not helping you. If a particular thought does not serve you, I want you to imagine a giant STOP sign each and every time you have that thought. Then I want you to replace that thought with one that is kind, true, and beneficial to you. This is much easier said than done. I started using this technique twenty years ago, and I am still not proficient. That is okay! The goal is to make progress over time.

Let's go through an example. This one is, again, from my own life. However, I suspect it resonates with a lot of parents. My son and I are both perfectionists. When I see him struggle with his perfectionism, I frequently blame myself. "It's my fault he's like this!" is a frequent thought I have. Was this thought created by my own brain? Yes, it was. Is that thought true? Nope. I didn't choose to be a perfectionist, and he didn't either. Did he inherit some perfectionist gene from me? Maybe, but that is outside of my control. I cannot choose the exact genetic makeup, or epigenetic expression, of my children's genome.

Finally, does this thought serve me? Of course not! I feel like crap when that thought enters my conscious awareness. I do my best to use my STOP sign technique. After stopping my thought, I tell myself, "My experience with perfectionism enables me to help my son work through it. We can figure this out." Is this replacement thought true? It sure is. After forty-plus years on this planet, I know a thing or two about living with perfectionism. Does this new thought serve me? Absolutely. Whenever I am faced with a challenging situation, I eventually figure it out. I believe that you can do the same.

Remember, the most common scenario of the CBT triangle is that thoughts lead to emotions, which in turn lead to actions. If you want to change your behaviors, you must first change the thoughts that are keeping you stuck, or diminishing your self-esteem, or are preventing you from living your best life.

Emotional Intelligence

While emotions are a personal experience, they are an integral aspect involved in our relationship with others. I'd like to introduce you to the concept of emotional intelligence. This concept involves using a certain skill set in order to relate to others and to communicate with others in an effective and constructive manner. Emotional intelligence involves perceiving, interpreting, appropriately evaluating, and utilizing emotions in a positive manner. This encompasses understanding and controlling the expression of personal emotions, as well as understanding, interpreting, and responding to the emotions of others.

Yikes, this is clear as mud. Let me summarize. Emotional intelligence involves becoming aware of our own emotions, as well as becoming aware of and understanding the emotions of others. It means that we can have empathy toward ourselves and others when it comes to the expression of emotions. It also involves being able to communicate our emotions and to have conversations with others about emotional matters.

Peter Salovey and John Mayer (no, not the singer) are credited with developing the term "emotional intelligence."[2] Again, psychologist Daniel Goleman developed a theory regarding the importance of emotional development, which is commonly abbreviated as EQ. He postulated five characteristics of high emotional intelligence:

- Self-awareness: understanding your behaviors, reactions to situations, and recognizing personal limitations
- Motivation: the pursuit of determination and self-drive
- Empathy: understanding and accepting the emotions of others, without judgment
- Self-regulation: the ability to acknowledge and manage your own emotions before reacting to a specific situation
- Social skills: the ability to listen to, communicate with, and engage others in communication while maintaining a sense of welcome

Emotional intelligence is important for numerous reasons. People with a high EQ tend to have strong leadership skills. They often motivate others, collaborate well in multiple situations, and reduce conflicts and misunderstandings. People with high EQ often learn from their mistakes, are able to remain calm in stressful situations, and build trusting relationships with others.

EQ is intrinsically related to IQ, or Intelligence Quotient. IQ involves intelligence; the total IQ score is determined by how well a person does on a standardized intelligence test. People with a high IQ have traditionally been called "smart." It's assumed that people with high IQs will be more successful than people with lower IQs, because high IQ has been linked to higher academic achievement, higher salaries, and higher work success.

However, that may not be the case. High EQ may be more relevant to determining strength of relationships, which can lead to success in the workplace. In fact, many schools are starting to incorporate social and emotional learning (SEL), or social and emotional learning, into their standard curriculum, which has been shown to improve academic performance because of its focus on building skills related to emotional intelligence.

Are any of these EQ skills achievable for children? Sure, in part. Every experience in a child's life is an opportunity to guide them toward the development of high emotional intelligence.

The best way to encourage your child to develop high emotional intelligence is to lead by example. Express your own emotions in a healthy manner. Be understanding and accepting of the emotions of others. If a child's friend bursts into tears during a playdate, comfort that child, and then talk to your child about how they could demonstrate empathy. Praise your child for listening to others without interrupting. Encourage frequent discussions about experiencing emotions and about appropriate behavioral expressions of those emotions. Develop strong social skills.

As I mentioned, when I was growing up, the preferred emotion was "fine," even though this isn't even a real emotion. Now that I am the mom, "fine" is not allowed in our home when my kids, husband, or I are acting the exact opposite of fine. Pretending to be fine when experiencing a strong emotion is counterproductive to the development of emotional intelligence.

One of the most important aspects of emotional intelligence that I introduced to my children was a very simple phrase: "How was your day?" I started asking them this question when they were far too young to truly understand its implications. Initially, my kids didn't answer. Yet, I persisted. Eventually, I was told "good."

When my children were preschoolers, I often followed this phrase by asking, "Did you do anything fun today?" When my children were school-age, the questions became more complex. "Did you learn anything cool today?" and "What was something that you wished you could change about your day?" were added to the mix.

The responses to those questions were not as important as the act of asking the questions. These days, my children often ask me, "How was your day?" before I can ask them the same question. They also ask their teachers, coaches, and friends how they are doing on a routine basis. Even better, my kids actually care to listen to the answer. Talk about proud Mama moments.

Each day, make sure to include a brief discussion of emotions in your child's daily routine. Remember, thoughts, feelings, and emotions are intimately related. Take the time to foster your child's emotional intelligence.

8

Attachment

Up to this point, we have primarily discussed emotions as an individual experience. Yet emotions are important in establishing relationships with others. One of the earliest emotional connections created between a caregiver and a child is called attachment. Attachment develops through the emotions and actions demonstrated by a caregiver toward an infant. Attachment is nonverbal, and it is not synonymous with love.

Infants are neurologically wired to form attachments with others. From an evolutionary standpoint, attachment is essential for an infant to survive. They look to others to meet their basic physical and emotional needs, because they are helpless in meeting their own needs. Attachments develop through everyday interactions with caregivers who assist the infant in getting their needs met.

However, it's not enough to simply attend to physical needs, such as providing food and changing diapers. The essence of attachment is emotion. This means that the quality of attachment varies based on how well a caregiver is able to respond to the child's nonverbal cues. The quality of these early relationships is essential, and attachment has huge implications for social, emotional, and cognitive development.

John Bowlby is credited with the development of attachment theory, though many influential psychologists expounded upon his initial work, including Ainsworth, Schaffer, and Emerson.[1] In this chapter, I am going to give you the cliff notes version.

There are two main types of attachment styles, secure and insecure. A secure attachment is the result of an infant who has a caregiver that is warmly and consistently responsive to their needs. This leads to a child who feels understood and safe; they believe in the goodness of relationships. Secure attachment has a profound impact on neurocognitive development. Secure attachment enables a child to develop a sense of trust and sets a foundation for the development of empathy, emotional regulation, self-awareness, problem-solving skills, and social skills.

There are several behaviors that caregivers can demonstrate in order to encourage the development of a secure attachment:

- Warmth and affection
- Responding to a child's wants and needs in a timely manner
- Being consistent and reliable
- Allowing a child to have the freedom to explore while observing from a safe distance
- Praising a child for who they are rather than what they do

Insecure attachment occurs when an infant perceives that their needs are not met. As a result, these kids grow up expecting that the relationships that they develop with others will involve some type of harm or abandonment. There are three categories of insecure attachment: avoidant, disorganized, and ambivalent or anxious.

Avoidant attachment occurs when a caregiver is distant and emotionally unavailable. These are caregivers who ignore or dismiss the child's needs. They ignore a child's cries, shame them for expressing fear, or act dismissive when a child is ill. As these children grow up, they have difficulty with intimacy. They struggle with expressing their thoughts and emotions to others. They often avoid getting involved in relationships, whether romantic or social.

Disorganized attachment occurs when a caregiver is consistently neglectful and/or abusive. Caregivers frequently employ yelling or intimidation in attempts to stop the child from expressing emotions. These are children who rely on caregivers who cause them distress or fear. As they grow up, they have a desire to be loved, yet avoid loving relationships in order to protect themselves.

Anxious attachment occurs when a caregiver is inconsistent; at times the caregiver is emotionally available and at other times, they are cold and distant. These are children who are never sure if their caregivers will provide for their needs or not. As a result, these are kids who grow up to crave closeness yet struggle to trust or rely on a partner. They may be open to intimacy but fear rejection from a partner.

The information about insecure attachment is here for completeness. The true focus is on understanding and developing secure attachment.

Here's how this plays out in real life. Let's say that seven-month-old Quinn starts crying in her playpen. You are on a work-related Zoom call and have a choice to make. You can excuse yourself for a moment to attend to her needs, or you can continue the call and ignore her until the call is over. As a working mom, I understand how challenging this situation may be. No one ever said parenting was easy! Time to be honest. The first scenario encourages secure attachment; the latter encourages insecure attachment.

Now imagine eight-month-old Elijah, who does not sleep through the night. He wakes up once between the hours of 11:00 p.m. and 7:00 a.m. because he wants to eat. Mom had been waking up to provide said nutrition but started to question herself when her mother-in-law determined that she was "spoiling" her child by providing food in the middle of the night. Continuing to feed Elijah in the middle of the night encourages secure attachment. Ignoring the cries of a hungry infant encourages insecure attachment.

Newsflash—you cannot spoil an infant by attending to their needs. Quite the opposite. It is essential that caregivers learn to respond to the physical and emotional needs of the infants that they are caring for. And these responses do not need to be perfect! I cannot tell you how many times I almost changed a dry diaper because my infant was crying and I didn't know what was wrong. Keep trying until you determine the unmet need. This encourages secure attachment.

Until six months of age, infants will coo, cry, smile, or scream to get almost anyone's attention in an attempt to get their needs met. At this young age, it doesn't matter if mom or grandparent or an older sibling changes their diaper; they just want the poop to be cleaned up. Similarly, when an infant is hungry, they will take a bottle from anyone who is willing to feed them. They slowly begin to differentiate between different caregivers. This sets the foundation for attachment figures, or people who infants attach to.

After six months of age, the attachment figure gains importance. At first, there is only a primary attachment figure. Around ten months of age, infants often have several attachment figures. They arrange these figures in a hierarchical manner. Some attachments will be stronger than others. It is very common for infants and young toddlers to cling to their attachment figures and cry when a non-attachment figure approaches.

As infants mature into toddlers, they become much more mobile. They are able to walk or run away from an attachment figure in order to explore their world. Yet they look to that attachment figure as a "safe base" to return to when they feel threatened or need comfort. Younger children with secure attachment tend to develop certain behaviors:

- They like to explore the world around them
- They are comfortable around others but prefer to be around their attachment figures
- They want attention and comfort from their attachment figures
- They are independent
- They develop strong social skills such as cooperation, compassion, taking turns, and sharing
- As they get older, they develop secure attachments with friends

It's very important to understand that attachment is not synonymous with love. A child does not somehow love their primary attachment figure more than they love the other caregivers in his or her life. They just have developed a relationship where they tend to look to a certain person to meet their needs and provide a sense of security. Attachment is not about love; it's about getting physical and emotional needs met.

I have had many parents, grandparents, and close family friends in my medical practice who are completely distraught because a child cried when separated from their primary attachment figure. This usually happens when a loved one wants to hold a child who subsequently starts crying and reaching for their primary attachment figure. This is not an indication of a lack of love or a rejection. It's simply a biologically driven mechanism of survival.

When my son was a young toddler, he developed an attachment to a wonderful woman named Chelsea, who was one of his daycare teachers. If Chelsea's shift ended before I was able to pick him up, Mason would cry uncontrollably until I arrived. He was familiar with the other daycare teachers, but he and Chelsea had an important emotional bond. If I wasn't around, he did not want to be separated from her.

My daughter went through a similar phase with a daycare provider named Karyn. The bond was so strong that we invited Karyn to Savannah's first birthday party. As soon as she arrived, Savannah made a beeline for Karyn. She was happy when held in Karyn's arms. When my parents arrived, Savannah cried when Karyn handed her over to my mom for a snuggle. My mom became upset, and I had to explain attachment to her. Honestly, she didn't get it. But I tried.

Attachment is not limited to child-caregiver relationships, and attachment does not end in childhood. Attachments continue to be important throughout a person's life and well into adulthood. Children who have secure attachments in early childhood are more likely to develop secure attachments as older children and adults.

The relationship with the primary attachment figure provides a framework for future relationship expectations. Kids who have experienced secure attachments early in life will have an easier time developing friendships and other relationships later in life. Be warm. Be nurturing. Be attentive to your child's needs and respond to those needs in a timely and emotionally responsive manner. Rest assured, none of these behaviors mean that you are spoiling your child.

PART III

PSYCHOSOCIAL DEVELOPMENT

9

Modeling

We have explored cognitive and emotional development. Before I switch gears and discuss psychosocial development, which refers to the development of personality and social skills, it's important to understand a concept called modeling. Children learn by watching the behaviors of the people in their life. What they see is what they will do. Your children will behave in the same way that you behave, whether you like it or not. This concept of modeling is also called observational learning.

If you want to encourage the development of synaptic pathways that lead to desirable behavior, you need to model appropriate behavior to your children. Whether you like it or not, your child has been constantly observing all of your actions since the day that they were born. They will watch the way that you interact with the world around you and assume that your actions are always correct and desired, at least when they are young.

Again, children do not possess the cognitive abilities to observe a behavior, interpret that behavior is appropriate or inappropriate, and identify a behavior deemed to be more positive in the future. This is a higher level frontal lobe skill that your child does not possess.

If you want your child to act in a certain way, you need to model that behavior for them. This means that you need to act in the exact manner that you want your child to act. You need to use the words that you want your child to use in their expression of language. You need to express your emotions in the same manner that you would prefer your child to express their own emotions. The reason that adopting a "Do as I say, not as I do" approach will fail miserably is because a child's brain is not developed enough to observe your actions, process them to determine if they are morally and socially appropriate, and then modify their own actions accordingly. Successful parenting involves leading by example.

I personally love a good cuss word. I don't swear at people, but I use swear words in my everyday conversations. I wasn't surprised when both of my children started saying the "F" word by the time they were three years old. Completely my fault—I had sworn in front of my children on many occasions.

As an adult, I know when, where, and how I can swear without it being problematic. Even if I am unaware of it, my self-control kicks in. My neocortex is well developed, and I have yet to scream "F*** you!" at anyone in my life. At the time, my toddlers did not have that ability. They did not understand how to appropriately use such a wonderful word in a socially acceptable manner.

My husband and I knew that expecting our kids to never swear while we continued to throw around four-letter words would fail miserably. My husband and I had a choice. We could keep swearing in front of the kids and prepare ourselves for endless phone calls from daycare teachers, or we could put the brakes on the four-letter words.

Bumblebees became our new F-word. It's got oomph and is totally harmless. And after a few months of intentionally not swearing in front of our kids, they stopped swearing. And as they got older and learned that swearing was not nice, they called us out on our behavior. I can't tell you how many times my kids have said, "Mommy! Language!" But this didn't happen when they were toddlers.

I know what you are thinking: But why didn't you just stop swearing altogether, even before your kids started talking? Because I am a swearer at heart. I love a good cuss word. I am willing and able to modify my behaviors for the benefit of my children. But I am not willing to sacrifice a part of who I am for them. I swear, I like to swear, and being a mommy does not mean that I have to stop swearing altogether. Parents do not need to sacrifice themselves for the sake of their child.

Let's get back to modeling. Again, children learn about the world by watching and experiencing the actions and behaviors of others around them. Everything you do or say in front of your child is a potential learning experience, whether you like it or not.

According to psychologist Albert Bandura, modeling involves four steps:

- Attention
- Retention
- Reproduction
- Motivation

Modeling occurs when someone watches the behavior of others, remembers that behavior, and imitates that behavior. The imitated behavior is more likely to be repeated if there is motivation to continue the behavior. Motivation involves an internal desire to act in a certain manner. Modeling does not require reinforcement, which is an external factor that encourages a desired behavior. However, reinforcement may lead to increased motivation.

Let's go through an example. In this example, you are the parent to three-year-old Grace. Today is laundry day, and Grace watches you fold a basket of laundry. You are both singing and laughing and making the most of this chore. The next day, you notice Grace trying to fold her blankets as she sings to her dolls. You praise her for being a big helper and notice that she actively seeks out participating in laundry day. Attention, retention, reproduction, and motivation.

If you want your child to be kind, you need to be kind. If you want your child to be respectful, you must act in a respectful manner toward others. Furthermore, if your child is engaging in unwanted behaviors, you need to determine if any of your behaviors are actually encouraging your child's unwanted behaviors to continue.

This takes a significant amount of self-awareness. Take a step back and observe. Are you engaging in a behavior that you do not want your child to engage in? If so, make a conscious effort to change your behavior. Finally, if your child is exhibiting a positive behavior that has been modeled to them, please praise your child! That praise will not directly encourage the behavior to continue, but it may increase your child's motivation.

10

Psychosocial Development of Infants, Toddlers, and Preschoolers

To me, the concept of personality is fascinating. The American Psychological Association (APA) defines personality as "individual differences in characteristic patterns of thinking, feeling, and behaving."[1] Clear as mud, right? Typically, personality is thought of as a set of personal characteristics and traits that encompass values, beliefs, abilities, and interests that contribute to subsequent behavior.

I'd like to introduce you to Erik Erikson, a psychologist who developed a theory involving eight stages of psychosocial development.[2] These stages encompass the entire lifespan, from birth to death, but in this chapter, we will focus on the first three stages. They span from infancy to five years old. Erikson categorized each one of these stages as having a specific conflict. Successful resolution of the conflict leads to the development of psychologically strong traits. The traits will shape personality and will affect behavior. It's important to note that successful resolution involves striking a balance between the two aspects of the conflict; this is not an all-or-none process.

Let me write that in a slightly different way. During each of Erikson's stages, a person faces a specific challenge (aka conflict), and the manner in which that challenge is resolved will shape personality. If the stage's conflict is successfully resolved, the psychological foundation for growth and development remains strong. On the other hand, if the stage's conflict is unresolved, it can affect a person in negative ways.

Remember the complexity of Piaget's theory? He developed a theory of cognitive development involving four distinct stages. Erikson's theory is even more complex. Again, the information presented is for completeness. I encourage you to focus on the stage of psychosocial development that your child is currently in. As your child grows up, you can refer to the next stage when it occurs.

Trust versus Mistrust

According to Erikson, the first stage of psychosocial development occurs from birth to approximately twelve months old. This stage involves the conflict of trust versus mistrust. Through life experiences, the infant is learning if they can trust the people around them. If the infant's caregivers are able to provide for their needs, demonstrate love and affection, and create a sense of stability and security, the infant will learn to trust the adults in their life. This sets the foundation for understanding that the world around them is also safe and dependable.

Is this sounding slightly familiar? Similar to attachment theory? Same same but different. I digress.

However, if during the first year of life, caregivers are unresponsive to the infant's physical, emotional, and social needs, that infant will fail to develop a sense of trust. Similarly, if the caregivers are inconsistent in meeting the needs of the infant, they are also at risk of developing a sense of mistrust. According to Erikson, these infants often became fearful. They learn that the world around them is inconsistent and unpredictable. Rather than developing a sense of security, they learn to view the world with apprehension.

It's important to note that the resolution of trust versus mistrust exists on a continuum. Successful development of trust means that infants are not fearful of experiences, given that their overall sense is one of security, yet they have a healthy wariness of potential danger.

In order to successfully resolve the conflict of trust versus mistrust, make sure to respond to your infant's needs. Feed them when they are hungry, change their diaper when wet or soiled, and provide comfort and affection frequently. You cannot spoil an infant; I cannot stress this enough. To ensure successful growth and development, your infant needs you to consistently respond to their needs.

At the same time, please understand that occasionally forgetting your diaper bag, and thus causing your child to sit in a wet diaper for an extra thirty minutes will not cause any harm. Likewise, failing to pick up your child the instant that they start crying will not doom them to go down the path of mistrust. It's the overall experience that matters the most. In my personal experience, if you are able to respond appropriately to your infant's needs at least 85 percent or more of the time, your infant will successfully navigate Erikson's first stage of psychosocial development. Please take this 85 percent concept with you through the remainder of Erikson's stages of psychosocial development.

Autonomy versus Shame and Doubt

The second stage of psychosocial development occurs from the ages of one to three years old. I like to think of the word "autonomy" to mean independence. Toddlers are starting to express their own desires and preferences. They want to do things without assistance, even though they may not yet possess the skills to act independently. Yet attempts at independent actions help the child to build self-confidence and a sense of personal control. Allowing a child to have choices and giving them the opportunity to make their own decisions (within reason) will help them to successfully complete this stage.

Shame involves an emotional state that indicates that a person is somehow wrong, unworthy, or bad. Children who are overly criticized or demeaned for their efforts at independence will be prone to self-doubt. Children who are overly controlled will be prone to feeling ashamed of their attempts at being autonomous. Unsuccessful resolution of this stage leads to a child who doubts themselves and the world around them. They will fear trying new things, lack confidence, and develop a sense of inadequacy.

Let's go through a few examples. A child who is trying to be autonomous will attempt to dress themselves. If a parent loses patience and decides to pull the child's pants on instead of giving the child a few more minutes to perform this act independently, this will foster a lack of autonomy. If a parent demands that a child eat chicken for lunch when the child does not like chicken, this encourages shame and doubt, because it negates the child's personal preferences.

In order to successfully resolve the conflict of autonomy versus shame and doubt, I suggest that parents allow their toddlers to have a voice in certain aspects of decision-making. To keep it simple and consistent, I usually recommend that parents give their toddlers two choices. For example, "Do you want strawberries or a banana with your lunch?" or "Do you want to wear your Batman pajamas or your Superman pajamas tonight?"

Offering a few reasonable choices encourages independence, as does allowing a child to explore a park, staying within eye distance of them but not hovering over them. In addition, it's important to praise a child for attempts at autonomous behavior, even if they fail. For example, tell them you are proud of them for the effort they put into getting dressed, even if they need your help.

Initiative versus Guilt

The third stage of psychosocial development occurs from ages three to five years old. The conflict is initiative versus guilt. Initiative involves engaging in new activities and exploring new experiences, as well as developing and executing plans. When a child has initiative, they are able to exert some control over their environment. As social skills are developing, initiative includes using skills during play and joining or creating activities with peers. This sets the foundation for future leadership skills.

Parents can help a child develop initiative by encouraging a child to try new things, encouraging attempts to explore the world around them, and helping guide the child toward making appropriate choices. For example, enrolling them in swim lessons or regularly taking them to a park to play helps a child develop initiative. When a child has initiative, they develop a sense of purpose and begin to develop resiliency.

On the other hand, guilt is the result of a child feeling embarrassed over failing to complete a task. Guilt may also be created when an adult, especially a parent, expresses irritation when a child makes a mistake. When parents prevent or discourage a child from engaging in imagination and play, guilt is the result.

Remember Piaget's theory of cognitive development? Imagination was a key feature at this age as well. Unfortunately, guilt causes a child to internalize mistakes, believing them to be a personal failure and an indication that the child is "bad." Parents who are dismissive, discouraging, or overly critical contribute to feelings of embarrassment and shame. Children who are unsuccessful at developing a healthy sense of initiative will often resist or fear trying new things. They may become overly dependent on others to help them.

Geez, that was a lot of information! Let's summarize. From birth to twelve months old, children thrive when their basic needs are met. They need love, affection, stability, and security. If this happens, the child will learn to trust others. From one to three years old, children need to be allowed to practice doing things for themselves. They benefit from being provided with choices and having their preferences respected, within reason. If this happens, the child will develop autonomy, or a sense of independence. From three to five years old, children need to be encouraged to use their imagination and engage in play. They need to be shown that mistakes are okay and that mistakes provide an opportunity for learning. If this happens, a child will develop initiative, or a willingness to engage in a new and possibly challenging activity. Trust, independence, and initiative are important aspects of personality. Remember, these are not all-or-none traits. They exist on a continuum.

I realize that this information is dense. Let's remember why this information is important. In order to parent our children more effectively, we need to understand their development. Erikson's theory of psychosocial development helps us to understand the challenges that our children face. We can utilize this information to help our children successfully resolve those challenges and allow for the growth of personality characteristics that foster success.

11

Psychosocial Development and the Importance of Play

When my nephew was three years old, he loved to take on the persona of other people. For a few weeks, he was convinced that he was Michael Jordan. He wore his Space Jam jersey everywhere! He assigned Space Jam characters to his mom, dad, and dog. I even have a video of him playing basketball in my driveway and telling me that his name is Michael, even though it isn't.

After he was finished being Michael Jordan, he transformed into Batman. My nephew was the ultimate crime-fighter. He would not take off his Batman cape and even insisted on wearing it to bed. Trees, non-Batman toys, and even my husband would suddenly morph in into the Joker, whom he would insist on fighting off. After the Batman phase, my nephew turned into a professional baseball player. He wore a batting helmet everywhere. He changed his persona every few weeks. This is pretend play at its finest, and it is actually very important for social development.

As adults, we rarely make time to play. Life is busy, and other responsibilities become higher priority. In fact, sometimes when adults play, they are often judged or ridiculed. I'm guilty of this as well. My husband enjoys playing some kingdom-building game on his cell phone. I have no idea what this game is called, nor do I understand the point of playing this game. More often than not, this annoys me because I feel like he could be doing something "more important." I try to remind myself that play is important, even for adults.

While play is important for people of all ages, adults don't need play in the same way that young children do. For children, play is essential. It is the foundation for psychosocial development. Play teaches children about themselves and about the world around them. Play also helps foster the development of many important skills. This, in turn, helps our children learn how to function as a member of a school community and sets the stage for future adult interactions.

If we can understand the importance of play, as well as the ways in which our children play, we can foster their social and emotional development. The great Fred Rogers once said, "Play is often talked about as if it were a relief from serious learning. But for children, play is serious learning. Play is really the work of childhood."[1]

If you don't know who Fred Rogers is, I encourage you to do a Google search of *Mister Rogers' Neighborhood*. It was a wonderful educational children's television show that ran from 1968 to 2001. The show was hosted by Fred Rogers, and he was truly ahead of his time. Play helps to develop a child's:

- Creativity and imagination
- Fine and gross motor skills
- Language and communication skills
- Sense of empathy
- Ability to cooperate, collaborate, and problem-solve
- Ability to manage emotions

It's important to understand that children play differently at different ages.

Remember our friendly psychologist, Jean Piaget? In addition to cognitive development, he had some thoughts about play. Children who are two to seven years of age, in the preoperational stage, engage in pretend play. They play in the realm of make-believe, and imagination is essential. This is where kids are playing or acting as if something is real even though it isn't. They use their imaginations to assign roles to other people or to inanimate objects, much like my nephew when he was Michael Jordan. Tea parties with teddy bears, digging for buried treasure in a sandbox, and zooming around as a superhero are all examples of pretend play.

Let me give you another example of pretend play. My daughter was very attached to her pacifier. When she was three years old, she was only allowed to have it for bedtime. Do I recommend that a three-year-old use a pacifier on a daily basis? Of course not, but my daughter is a force to be reckoned with. As always, as a mom, I pick my battles and did the best that I could at the time.

During the day, Savannah put her pacifier on her nightstand. And every night, she ran to her bedroom, grabbed her pacifier, and cradled it in her hands. She rocked her hands back and forth, saying, "Oh nookie, how was your day? How are you? I missed you!" She acted like her pacifier was a beloved friend, even though it was an inanimate object.

Please do not discourage pretend play. It's not silly or immature. Quite the opposite; this type of play fosters social, emotional, and cognitive development. Pretend play also helps build language skills, encourages creativity, and helps to develop problem-solving skills. Provide your preoperational child with props and costumes. Allow your child to be creative, even if it means getting messy. Welcome your child's imaginary friend into your home. Take the time to play school or super heroes or fairy princesses with your child. If you are able to fully engage in pretend play with your child, I guarantee it will bring you and your child so much joy.

Let's take this concept of play even deeper. Mildred Parten was a psychologist who postulated six stages of play, based on age.[2] As with most theories created prior to the twenty-first century, it is based on "typical" or "normal" children, whatever that means. Even though this theory does not account for neurodivergence, I find it to be helpful in a lot of ways. The stages of play that I am about to describe are not limited to the specific age range that Parten initially associated the stage with, and the stages of play can overlap. Finally, it's important to note that once a child masters a stage, they may often return to it as older children and even adults.

The first stage of play is called unoccupied play and occurs from birth to about three months of age. Parten called it unoccupied play. During this stage, there is no social interaction, and use of language is almost nonexistent. Examples of unoccupied play include a baby who shakes a rattle or giggles at an object hanging from a baby play mat.

Parten's second stage of play is called solitary play. It occurs from three months to two and a half years of age. Solitary play continues for longer periods of time than unoccupied play does. In addition, solitary play is more focused than unoccupied play. However, lack of interest in other people is still a common feature of solitary play. Again, this is normal and developmentally appropriate! Please don't expect younger toddlers to show an interest in playing with other children. At the same time, it's important to allow them opportunities to observe the behavior of other children their age.

The third stage of play is called observer or onlooker play. This stage occurs around three to three and a half years old. This is where a child will watch other children play but does not participate in the activity. Imagine a child who is at a park, watching other kids play while standing at a distance. Kids in the observer stage are starting to become interested in the play behaviors of other kids but don't actively try to play with those children.

Parents often worry that a child in the observer stage is shy or socially awkward. They aren't! Children in this stage of play are acutely aware of the actions of the people around them. Through observation, children learn about following the rules of a game, cooperation with other people, and strengthening their attention span and memory skills. Every time that you attend a sporting event or watch one on TV, you are engaging in observer play. Watching your child's band concert or their tennis match is another form of observer play.

Observer play may overlap with the next stage of play, called parallel play. Children ages three and a half to four and a half years engage in this stage. In this type of play, children play side by side with other kids but are actually playing alone. They may utilize the same toys, yet are still playing independently. An example is two children who are building two different towers out of the same set of blocks or two children who are sitting at the same table but coloring different pictures. At this age, kids do not try to influence the behavior of others. They simply play in their own world, participating in the same activities as their peers, physically near other kids their age.

Parallel play is awesome, but it can be disconcerting for some parents until they understand it. Please do not panic if you arrange a play date for your toddler only to watch them ignore the other child completely! This is age-appropriate behavior. Similar to onlooker learning, children who engage in parallel play are learning about social interaction by observing the world around them. They just do so in closer proximity to other children and engaging in play activities.

As a child moves from the toddler to preschool years, they start to engage in something called associative play. This tends to happen between three and a half and four years old. Associative play is where children are playing together but not working toward a common goal. There may be brief cooperation such as sharing a toy or riding a tricycle in the same direction. An example of associative play is children who are playing kitchen, but one child is making pizza and the other is making French fries for their baby doll.

When those brief moments of cooperation occur during associative play, make sure to praise your child. This will help the desired behavior continue. However, please do not expect your child to share toys consistently at this age. They are still learning about sharing. If another child takes their toy, they are not likely to let it go without a fight. Don't panic; they will eventually progress to cooperative play, where sharing occurs on a more regular basis.

Cooperative play does not typically occur until a child is four and a half years old. This type of play involves children playing together while working toward a common goal. Examples of cooperative play include putting a puzzle together or playing duck, duck, goose.

Cooperative play is the type of play that most people think of when they talk about children playing together.

Conflict can arise during cooperative play, and this is normal! Remember, preschoolers are still dealing with egocentrism. Being able to engage in cooperative play sets the stage for being able to interact successfully in social settings such as school and in sports.

Why is this important? Because it helps parents to set appropriate expectations for their child. Identifying the stage of play that the child is in helps a parent to encourage behaviors that are specific to that stage, which fosters development. Please, don't get caught up in the age ranges. It's also important to remember that these stages of play overlap. Finally, know that Parten's work is a theory, not absolute fact.

Let's go through an example. The children are between three and four years old, and they are playing in a large sandbox at a daycare. Many of the children are playing side by side, yet some children are filling a bucket with sand, while others are digging in the sand. This is parallel play. A few children briefly work together to attempt to build a sandcastle. This is cooperative play. Yet another child is sitting in the sand, watching the children around him. This is observer play.

All of these styles of play are developmentally appropriate. A person who doesn't understand Parten's theory may be upset that not all of the children are building a sandcastle together. This is trying to force a style of play upon children who are not developmentally ready for it.

Is this starting to make sense? Understanding developmentally and age-appropriate aspects of play allows parents to encourage and strengthen social skills instead of hindering those skills by holding on to unrealistic expectations.

12

Psychosocial Development of Older Children

Play continues to be an important aspect of psychosocial development as children enter school age. The ages of six to eleven years old are often referred to as middle childhood. These children are still working on developing strong cooperative play skills. At times, they may pick dandelions in right field during a coach-pitch baseball game instead of paying attention to the game itself. They may yell at a teammate who is not playing by the rules.

Engaging in cooperative play helps children learn how to work together. It improves communication abilities; children learn to express their needs and desires while listening to the needs and desires of others. Cooperative play allows children to practice negotiation and conflict resolution, which are emerging skills at this age. In addition, cooperative play helps the development of empathy; children start to think about the perspective of others in order to make sure the game is fair for everyone.

Industry versus Inferiority

Do you remember our friend Erik Erikson? Again, he developed a theory of psychosocial development. The conflict of industry versus inferiority occurs between six and eleven years old. Industry refers to the ability to work hard in attempts to achieve something. Hard work is valued because the effort involved typically leads to something greater in the end. As these school-age children are learning physical, social, and emotional skills, they need the support and encouragement of the adults in their life. The concept of industry is dependent upon the feelings of competence, which hopefully were achieved in the previous stages of psychosocial development. It's important to focus on the effort that a child demonstrates, rather than the outcome of their behavior.

Once a child enters the school system, their skills and achievements are measured in an objective manner. Grades, hitting a home run, and the ability to make friends are all measurable achievements. This objectivity allows kids to pay attention to the quality of their work. Children who are encouraged by their parents and teachers develop a belief in their ability to perform tasks, which in turn strengthens their sense of self. Supportive relationships with parents, teachers, friends, and other loved ones can help develop positive self-esteem, which can lead to self-confidence.

If children in this stage are not encouraged to attempt new skills or perform complex tasks by parents or teachers, they may develop a sense of inadequacy. This leads to feelings of self-doubt; the child may feel that their abilities do not measure up to those of their peers. Examples of this include a child who is told that they are not the "smart sister" or a child who is not allowed to take a karate class because they are presumed to lack discipline. Should a child fail to develop industry, they may be less likely to try new things, for fear of failure or scrutiny. This creates a sense of inferiority and can lead to lower self-esteem.

Friendships become prevalent during middle childhood and provide a significant influence on a child's psychosocial development. Such relationships help children learn rules related to appropriate social behaviors. Children in middle childhood are becoming more proficient in seeing the point of view of others. During the later stages of middle childhood, friends confide in each other, sharing thoughts or feelings that they don't tell others. They help each other solve problems and are often supportive and caring. These relationships are important and should not be trivialized.

It is so hard as a parent to allow our kids to be friends with a child that we don't like! With all due respect, as a parent, you need to check yourself. It's important to trust your child and their developing opinions. If their so-called friend is a negative influence, your child will eventually figure it out. An industrious child will not want to continue a friendship with someone who tries to bring them down. At the same time, if your child's friend is engaging in questionable or dangerous behaviors, it's important for you as a parent to step in and intervene. Talk about the importance, and challenge, of balance!

Please remember that industry and inferiority are not mutually exclusive. Many times, a child in this stage will feel confident about some of their abilities and a bit inadequate about other abilities. Helping a child to successfully navigate this stage involves providing them with unconditional love and support. Again, it's important to focus on the effort that the child puts forth, rather than the outcome. In fact, focusing on, and praising, the effort a child puts forth is perhaps the most essential aspect of parenting a child during middle childhood.

At the same time, it's important to be realistic. Don't overly inflate your child's ego. Don't tell them that they are going to be the next Tom Brady. Don't suggest that they are the smartest fourth grader that you have ever met. This approach focuses on outcome, not effort. Let's be real. It's also dishonest. Help your child to understand their strengths and weaknesses. Allow your child to express themselves and actually listen to them. Finally, provide emotional support if they fail to live up to their expectations or the expectations of others. Be a source of strength and comfort for your child.

Identity versus Role Confusion

From twelve to eighteen years of age, children are navigating the conflict of identity versus role confusion. As teenagers are trying to figure out who they are and how they relate to the world around them, they may take on different roles and gender identities, and adopt changing behaviors. Teenagers are trying to figure out who they are as a person and what they want to do with their life. They may try out different personas to see what fits best. They may be highly influenced by their friends and may push their parents away.

As hurtful as this may be, it's important to give teenagers the opportunity to explore. It's good for their development to challenge dogma and belief systems. Do not take this opposition as a personal attack against you or against your beliefs. Instead, reframe your thinking to allow a difference of opinions. At the same time, do not try to force your child to adopt the exact same belief system that you have. Encourage open discussions and allow your teenager to ask questions. Listen carefully to their ideas and beliefs without judgment or condemnation. Give them grace and allow them to explore different belief systems while maintaining your own personal beliefs.

Teenagers who are not allowed to explore different relationships, beliefs, and values may feel confused about their place in life. They may be unsure about who they are and how they fit into the world. Teenagers without a strong sense of identity may struggle with commitment. They may lack confidence in themselves and in their abilities.

Furthermore, teenagers who are forced to conform to their parents' ideas and values often develop role confusion. They will have trouble figuring out who they are and/or struggle with determining their place in society. These are teenagers who become adults that are more concerned about pleasing their parents than becoming the person they were meant to be. As a result, these teenagers who turn into adults who feel incomplete. I certainly don't want that for my kids, and I hope you don't want that for yours either.

Successful parenting of a teenager requires a delicate balance of allowing independence and experiences yet doing your best to ensure your child's safety. You need to love them enough to let them spread their wings and try to fly. You may need to throw them out of the nest, you may need to rescue them before they crash to the ground, but to a certain extent, you need to let them figure certain things out on their own. Yet, at the same time, it's important to be a consistent source of love and support.

The teenage years are often when dating becomes important, and intimate relationships start to develop. As a parent, it is important to understand that the emotions involved with teenage love are very real. Please don't dismiss these relationships as unimportant or unsustainable. This will create a roadblock to communication. Or worse, your dismissal may make the relationship more desirable to your child. A teenager may try harder to stay in a relationship, even if it is unhealthy, just to prove you wrong.

Dating is a normal part of the psychosocial development of teenagers. Please don't forbid your sixteen-year-old from dating. This will actually be detrimental to their development. In addition, resist the urge to judge your teenager's date/significant other as "not good enough" for them. Rather, give that person a chance and get to know them. Ask your teen about the positive attributes that they see in them. If you get to know your teenager's date/significant other and still don't like them, keep it to yourself. Don't speak negatively about that person in front of your child. That being said, if the relationship seems unhealthy, you need to speak up. Even teenagers can become involved in abusive relationships.

Finally, please resist the urge to tell your child, "Because I said so!" This stifles their development. Remember, your teenagers are looking to you for guidance more than you realize. Their actions may indicate otherwise, but you are still the most important role model in their life.

Again, lots of information in this chapter! Let's summarize. From ages six to eleven years old, children are grappling with the conflict of industry versus inferiority. If children are encouraged to try new things, are supported in developing and believing in their abilities, and are praised for the effort that they apply, they will develop a sense of industry. Let me write that again, in a slightly different manner. If you want your school-age child to thrive, allow them to explore new experiences. Focus on the effort they put forth, rather than the outcome of their actions. Encourage social interactions with peers.

Let's go through an example. Sam is a nine-year-old who is struggling in school, and with math specifically. His parents have had very good communication with Sam's teacher, and they have created a strategy to help Sam feel good about his efforts. Sam's parents help him with his homework, yet refuse to do that homework for him. Over time, Sam learns to try his best and is happy about how hard he is trying, as are his parents and teacher.

Olivia is a classmate of Sam. She is also nine years old but struggles with reading. Her parents are highly educated and cannot understand Olivia's disdain for reading. Olivia's parents have high expectations for her yet have a low tolerance for what they consider to be disobedience. When Olivia refuses to complete her reading homework, her parents yell at her. They demand that she read for twenty minutes a night yet show no interest in reading with her. They assume that she should be self-motivated to read.

Sam is much more likely to resolve the conflict of industry versus inferiority than Olivia is. Sam has support from his parents, commitment from his parents to communicate with his teacher, and a knowledge that effort is more important than outcome. On the other hand, Olivia's parents are not supportive of her emerging skills. Their expectations do not match her current ability level. They are more concerned with their image than they are with helping their struggling child make progress in school.

Let's go through another example. Luke is a sixteen-year-old male. He is on the varsity basketball team and was voted homecoming king. His girlfriend adores him. Overall, he is happy with his life and wants to be the best that he can be. He struggled with academics in the past. In fact, at one point, his grades were so bad that he was almost ineligible to participate in sports. This was disappointing to his parents, who are both highly educated. Rather than yell at Luke for his poor grades, his parents arranged for a tutor. With the extra academic support, he is on track to graduate with a solid GPA. College is in his future, and he aspires to be an engineer. Because his parents have provided consistent love, support, and help, Luke is thriving.

On the other hand, Hunter is an incredibly intelligent fifteen-year-old who lacks parental support. Because he is so intelligent, other kids pick on him. By the time he got to middle school, he was being bullied on a daily basis. His parents felt that Hunter's response to the bullying was "weak" and encouraged him to toughen up. Eventually Hunter stopped talking about the bullying. He became more and more isolated. His grades started to slip, and because of this, his parents frequently yelled at him. Unfortunately, his parents didn't realize how much Hunter was struggling, socially and emotionally, until he attempted suicide.

These examples are based on real patients of mine. The kids had very similar economic situations. They lived in the same community and went to the same schools. The main difference between Sam and Olivia, and between Luke and Hunter, was the way they were raised. Sam and Luke's parents chose to parent the child that they had. Olivia and Hunter's parents chose to parent the child they wish they had.

PART IV

TEMPERAMENT

13

Understanding Temperament and Goodness of Fit

In the previous chapters, we have focused on children at certain ages and developmental stages in very general terms. It's time to go deeper. In the next few chapters, you will get to know your child (or each of your children) on a more personal level. I want to introduce you to the concept of temperament.

Have you ever wondered why two people have different reactions to the exact same situation? The reason is something called temperament. Temperament is often defined as the way in which people organize their behavioral and emotional response to the world around them. If you can understand your child's unique temperament and adjust your parenting strategies based on your child's unique temperament, it will completely change your life for the better.

Temperament is something innate, meaning something that a person is born with. Certain aspects of temperament can change over time; more on that later. Rather than trying to modify a person's temperament, we become more effective parents if we can understand our child's unique temperament and work within that construct.

In 1956, Alexander Thomas and Stella Chess ran a thirty-year longitudinal study related to aspects of temperament called the New

York Longitudinal Study of Child Temperament.[1] They determined that there are nine attributes that make up temperament. It's important to note that none of these attributes are inherently good or bad; they just are.

- *Activity Level*: people with a high activity level have trouble sitting still. They enjoy movement. People with a low activity level prefer less noise, less movement, and more sedentary activities.

- *Intensity*: to me, would be more accurately referred to as the expression of emotional intensity. People with high intensity express intense emotions. People with low intensity may experience intense emotions, yet they express their emotions in a more subdued manner.

- *Approachability*: relates to people's initial reactions to newness. People with high approachability are eager to experience new people, places, or things. People with low approachability are hesitant with such experiences and tend to withdraw.

- *Adaptability*: involves how easily a person adapts to transitions. A person with high adaptability transitions between activities with ease and does not require much time to feel comfortable in new situations. A person with low adaptability struggles with transitions and initially is very hesitant of change to their current situation.

- *Distractibility*: refers to the level of concentration or focus. People with high distractibility have difficulty concentrating and are easily distracted by sounds, sights, or feelings of discomfort. People with low distractibility can easily maintain focus in a variety of situations despite any outside stimuli.

- *Sensitivity*: describes a person's response to physical stimuli. People with high sensitivity are bothered by stimuli that pertain to the five senses. Examples of this include picky eating, struggles to sleep in a room that is too warm or cold, or refusal to wear clothes that are itchy. People with low sensitivity are not bothered by loud noises or by flashing lights. They like to try new foods.

- *Regularity (or Rhythmicity)*: relates to how predictable bodily functions are. People with high regularity have regular habits when it comes to appetite, sleeping and elimination. People with low regularity are the opposite, with unpredictable appetite, sleeping and elimination habits.

- *Persistence*: involves the duration of time that a person can continue activities when there are challenges or obstacles. People with high persistence continue the activity when obstacles arise without getting overly frustrated. They also tend to practice a skill they want to master. People with low persistence will abandon an activity when obstacles arise. They are easily frustrated by challenging activities.

- *Mood*: relates to the way a person reacts to the world, either positively or negatively. A person with a high mood is generally happy and reacts to the world in a positive manner. A person with a low mood is more serious and downtrodden.

I know that was a lot of information. You do not need to memorize any of this. Come back to it anytime you need; it is here as a reference.

Do not view any of these attributes as being limited to high or low. They each exist on a continuum; there is a range from low to average to high. This is essential to understand. In addition, please do not assume that high is better than low and vice versa. That's simply not the case. There are no "bad" attributes of temperament. Certain attributes may be easier to deal with, but that doesn't make them inherently better or worse.

I want to warn you that attempts have been made to group the above nine attributes into three categories: "easy," "slow to warm," and "difficult." I suspect this was done because it makes the information easier to comprehend. I will not mince words. Based on my experience, these three categories are actually harmful; they are not only judgmental, but they oversimplify the complex nature of temperament. Please, ignore these terms when it comes to temperament.

Let's go through an example. My husband and I playfully refer to our daughter Savannah as "pokey puppy." It's as if she exists in a different time plane, and it has always been this way. She dawdles and oftentimes lacks a sense of urgency. We could be running late to an event, and she will suddenly exclaim, "I have to go the bathroom!" While most of the time it is just a quirky part of who she is, at times it can be problematic.

If my husband and I chose to parent the punctual child we wanted, we would demand that Savannah hurry up. We might make her leave the house before she finished eating her breakfast. This would inevitably lead to yelling, resistance, and possibly even a temper tantrum. But my husband and I know better. If we have to be somewhere at a certain time, we wake Savannah up early. If she is still eating breakfast when it is time to leave, we bring that breakfast in the car for her. My husband and I adjust our parenting strategies based on our child's unique temperament.

Alexander Thomas and Stella Chess also coined the term "goodness of fit" when it comes to temperament. If a child's trait is compatible with their parents' same trait, that is goodness of fit. Compatibility does not mean possessing the exact same degree of a temperament trait. That is a huge misconception.

In fact, it is often the similarity of traits that causes discord in a parent-child relationship. For example, let's imagine a mom and her daughter who both have high levels of regularity. Remember, regularity relates to bodily functions such as appetite. The child with high regularity is hungry for dinner at 5:00 p.m., but the mom with high regularity serves the family dinner every evening at 6:00 p.m. sharp. If the mom is insistent that everyone in the family eat dinner together, exactly at 6:00 p.m., there is going to be significant conflict. This is the opposite of goodness of fit. Remember, we cannot change attributes of temperament. Within this highly regular family, it would be helpful to consider allowing the child to eat when she is hungry, rather than at the time the mom prefers to serve dinner.

There are two aspects of goodness of fit: how the trait affects interactions with the environment itself and how the trait affects interactions with the people around them. When the qualities of the environment match a person's temperament and abilities, that is a good fit. For example, when a person with average to low sensitivity experiences a thunderstorm, they are not fazed by it. That's a good fit. However, for a person with high sensitivity, a thunderstorm will likely trigger significant anxiety and maybe even a temper tantrum. That indicates a lack of goodness of fit.

Oftentimes, we cannot control the environment around us. As it relates to temperament, it's not so much about modifying the environment but rather guiding our children through experiences that lack goodness of fit.

Let's go back to the previous example. Parenting a child with high sensitivity through a loud thunderstorm involves providing support and comfort. That's how to parent the child you have. On the other hand, chastising or punishing a child who is crying during a thunderstorm is a way to parent the child you want, and it's not something that I recommend.

When the expectations of the people in the child's life match the child's temperament, that is also a good fit. For example, imagine a parent who enjoys attending a variety of social engagements. Having a child with high approachability would lead to goodness of fit, as the child would enjoy new experiences and meeting new people. However, having a child with low approachability would likely lead to conflict and even problematic behavior if the parent tried to force them to socialize with someone they had never met before.

Does this mean that you never take a child with low approachability to social engagements for fear of them getting upset? Of course not! It just means that we adjust our expectations and provide love and support during times that may cause stress.

I have an important caveat. I need you to take judgment out of the term "goodness." Simply being a good fit does not inherently make it better than something that lacks goodness of fit. If it were up to me, "goodness of fit" would actually be called "compatibility of fit." No one asked me, so goodness of fit is what we have.

Understanding goodness of fit has several benefits. It helps you to understand your child's behavior. You can use this information to help your child understand their interactions with the world around them and help them manage their reactions. You can assist your child choose activities that would probably be enjoyable to them, instead of the activities you want them to participate in.

In addition, understanding goodness of fit will help you create a deeper understanding of your child and often leads to increased empathy. It will help you develop more realistic expectations for your child and for their behavior. This in turn will lead to higher quality parent-child relationships. In the next chapter, we explore each trait of temperament in more detail. Then we turn our attention to the ways in which we can utilize goodness of fit within the context of our parenting strategies.

14

Attributes of Temperament

It's time to take a deep dive into the nine attributes of temperament. Remember that these traits are innate; your child did not choose to have them. As we explore each trait, I will be giving examples from my children, as it can help you apply the traits to your own children.

Activity Level

Children who have a high activity level need to physically move and often struggle to sit still. They also talk a lot. A child with a high activity level may not be able to sit through an entire family dinner. If a parent is understanding of this and willing to make accommodations, dinner will be much more pleasant for everyone in the home. Kids with a high activity level often gravitate toward sports such as soccer, football, or basketball. If their parent also has a high activity level, this often leads to goodness of fit. These are families who would benefit from taking walks or bike rides together. They can go on vacations that involve skiing or swimming or scuba diving.

Children with a low activity level are not necessarily destined to be couch potatoes. They simply tend to be more relaxed and gravitate toward more sedentary activities. They may love to read, which is awesome! They prefer less noise and may be overwhelmed at a park that is packed with other kids who are running around and screaming. Lower activity levels are often desired in the school setting because these are kids that are more likely to sit in their seat and keep their hands to themselves.

My son and I have high activity levels; my husband and daughter have average activity levels. Movie night in our house is quite the experience. My son constantly asks questions about what may come next, he comments on the current scene, he gets up from the couch and moves around. Sometimes it is hard to hear the movie because of his talking. I need to be doing something else during the movie; I write, I get up twenty times to do the dishes or clean the kitchen or refill the popcorn tub. My husband and daughter often get frustrated with me and my son because we disrupt the movie with our movement and talking. They can easily sit and relax while the movie is playing. My son and I, not so much.

Intensity

Children who have high-intensity experience and express big emotions. These are the kids who scream at the TV when their favorite football team is losing, cry when you are out of their favorite cereal, or shriek with excitement when they see a puppy. High-intensity kids may be more prone to have temper tantrums well beyond the toddler years. People with high-intensity experience, and express, the highest of highs and the lowest of lows.

On the other hand, children who have low intensity display their emotions in a much more subdued way. They may not display external expressions of emotion. It's important to understand that people with low intensity still experience emotions, often just as deeply as people who have high intensity. They may need more assistance in expressing their emotions; you don't want to ignore these kids just because their reactions are muted.

Developing emotional regulation is an important skill for anyone to have. You don't want your high-intensity kid to lose their first job because they screamed at their boss. Likewise, you don't want your low-intensity kid to bury their feelings for years and years until they explode. Understanding your child's intensity can help you guide them through the ups and downs of life.

My son has high intensity. My daughter has moderately low intensity. Dinnertime was always an interesting experience in our house when my kids were toddlers. If I offered my son food he did not want, we all knew about it. He would scream or throw that food on the floor. It was very easy for my husband and me to understand my son's displeasure. On the other hand, my low-intensity daughter remained quiet and simply refused to eat. She said nothing and did not ask for different food. As she became older, we could ask her about her food refusal. She would usually cry but not admit that she didn't have a taste for the food unless we specifically asked her if she wanted something different to eat.

Approachability

Children with high approachability are not afraid to try new things. In fact, they often welcome unfamiliar situations. They enjoy meeting new people, going to new places, and are more open to trying new foods. These are the kids that may be described as "adventurous." If your child has high approachability, you are probably going to need to have multiple conversations about stranger danger. You may need to remind them repeatedly about not running away from you to explore a new place. You will have to be cautious about them opening the front door when someone rings your doorbell.

Children with low approachability are hesitant with novelty. They are the kids who cling to their moms when taken to a new playground. They will cry if they are dropped off at a new daycare. If your child has low approachability, you may need to arrive at a new place early in order for your child to feel comfortable. You may need to introduce them to new people instead of expecting them to introduce themselves. You may need to be understanding when your child refuses a hug from Aunt Sally, whom they haven't seen in three years.

My daughter has low approachability. When she was invited to one of her friend's seventh birthday party, she clung to me for a good fifteen minutes after we arrived. Her best friend lives six houses away from us. They play together outside of school on a weekly basis, at a minimum. They have frequent sleepovers. In addition, my daughter knew every single guest at the party. They were her classmates, many of whom live in our subdivision. Yet, she was hesitant to engage. No amount of reassurance from me was helpful. She just needed time to adapt. Once she was comfortable, she ran off with her friends and completely ignored me for hours. But it took some time.

Simply by understanding, and working with, my child's approachability trait, she was able to enjoy the birthday party. Had I left immediately, before she was acclimated to her surroundings, I guarantee you she would have been in tears, begging to go home. Am I happy that my daughter has low approachability? Not really, but that is a part of who she is, so my feelings about it are irrelevant. I'm committed to working within the framework of my child's temperament, and I encourage you to do the same.

Adaptability

Adaptability is all about how a person responds to transitions, meaning how quickly they adapt to a change in activity. Children with high adaptability navigate transitions easily. Once they have been introduced to a new situation, they become comfortable quickly. They can handle change and easily move from one activity to the next without difficulty. These are the kids who don't struggle when they unexpectedly have a substitute teacher or if they are late to the bus stop and suddenly have to be driven to school. They can move from recess back to class without having a meltdown.

Children with low adaptability struggle with transitions. They take more time to become comfortable in a new situation. These are the kids who want to keep playing with Play-Doh when it is time to clean up for lunch. They may even throw a temper tantrum when you put that Play-Doh away. In addition, children with low adaptability often prefer routines and benefit from knowing what to expect. It is helpful to give warnings before a new activity or a change in location occurs. Kids with low adaptability may need five different warnings before a transition is about to occur. That's okay.

When it comes to transitions, I happen to love the strategy of setting alarms. Both of my kids have a fairly high adaptability level, but even so, I want my home to run as smoothly as possible. Whenever I need to transition my kids from one activity to another, I consider setting a timer. In fact, I usually tell our Alexa device to set a timer for a certain number of minutes and then I tell my kids what that timer indicates. If my kids need to take a shower, or do homework, or brush their teeth, I consider setting an alarm after telling them about the transition that is about to occur. This works great in our home.

Distractibility

Distractibility involves how easily people can be prevented from paying attention to something. People with high distractibility struggle with inattention. They easily lose focus and have a hard time completing multi-step tasks without frequent reminders. These are the kids who will look out the window at another class participating in recess when they are supposed to be taking a test. They will struggle to help their friends build a sandcastle in the sandbox, because they get distracted by the kids who are using the swings instead of playing in the sand.

People with low distractibility can sustain their attention on whatever task they are involved with. They can ignore the beep of a car horn while they are doing their homework. They can brush their teeth, wash their face, and put on their pajamas when you ask them to instead of doing a dozen other things. Kids with low distractibility will do something the first or second time you ask them, especially if it is something they want to do. These are the kids that pay attention to their teacher, often complete their chores with a few reminders, and may seem more compliant than kids with higher distractibility, even though that is not the case.

I have a word of caution about distractibility. The ability to sustain attention develops over time. Even a person with low distractibility likely had an attention span of about several nanoseconds when they were a toddler. If you have young children, please don't stress about this attribute. Make a mental note to put it in the "to be determined" pile and come back to it later. Ideally, the degree of distractibility is determined once a person's brain is fully developed.

However, if you have an older child with high distractibility, they may need frequent reminders to complete a task, such as cleaning their room or finishing their homework. They may benefit from placing written checklists of their chores on the refrigerator door. They may need you to use alarms to keep them on track. Most of all, kids with high distractibility do best when their parents are patient with them. They are not trying to stray from the task at hand. They are not trying to be difficult. As with all things related to temperament, it's just a part of who they are.

It's also important to note that children with high distractibility do not necessarily meet diagnostic criteria for ADHD, or attention deficit hyperactivity disorder. Distractibility is an attribute of temperament. ADHD is a medical diagnosis that is made by an appropriate healthcare provider.

When my son was younger, he had high distractibility. On school days, when I asked him to put his shoes on and grab his backpack before walking to the bus stop, he usually stopped to pet the dogs first. I needed to remind him to stop petting the dogs and put on his shoes. After a second reminder, he usually put on his shoes but may have forgotten to grab his backpack before walking to the bus stop. As he has gotten older, his distractibility level has decreased. Don't get me wrong, he is still on the higher end of the distractibility continuum. I still need to ask him two to three times to put his shoes on before school. That's okay. It has become a part of our morning routine.

Sensitivity

This attribute involves the five senses—taste, touch, sight, smell, and hearing. Children with high sensitivity are easily upset by loud noises, bright lights, and certain smells. They may want the tags cut out of their clothes or they may get nauseous and vomit when they experience a strong smell that they do not like. These are children who may have a giant temper tantrum if they experience sensory overload.

Children with high sensitivity can be challenging. Please remember that they did not choose this attribute. Be willing to make accommodations for them. This may mean that you need to watch the Fourth of July fireworks on TV instead of taking your child to a live event. You may need to open the windows when you are cooking food they do not like. You may need to buy them noise-cancelling headphones to wear on the school bus if it is too loud.

On the other hand, children with low sensitivity are not easily bothered by strong sensations. They don't cover their ears when you vacuum, they will not complain about the smell of your cooking, and they don't refuse to use the soap you buy because of the way it feels on their skin. They tend to be pretty mellow when it comes to experiencing any one of the five senses.

In my experience, sensitivity is much more complex than it was initially described. Not all kids have the same level of sensitivity to each of the five senses. A child may have a high sensitivity to sound but a lower sensitivity to touch. Another child may have a high sensitivity to smell but a lower sensitivity to taste. I have no scientific studies to back this assertion; it's all based on my observations from over a decade of caring for children.

The original theory of temperament did not account for this variability, but I encourage you to do so. For example, my son has a high sensitivity when it comes to certain tastes, but not to sound. I have to buy him Tanner's Tasty Paste vanilla cupcake-flavored toothpaste in order for him to brush his teeth appropriately. He refuses to use any minty-flavored toothpaste. Yet he is never bothered by loud noises. In fact, he is the absolute loudest person I know. I love him deeply, but damn. If I had a dollar for every time I had to ask him to quiet down, I'd own a private island by now.

My daughter is highly sensitive to sound yet has a low sensitivity to touch. She hates loud noises and sometimes wears noise-cancelling headphones when she is on the school bus. Yet she loves having her scalp massaged, her back rubbed, and will give you the biggest, strongest hug you have ever received. I strongly encourage you to treat each of the five senses individually. Apply the concept of sensitivity to each of the senses, one by one.

Regularity

I'll be the first to admit that regularity is most likely the most uncomfortable attribute of temperamental traits to think about; who actually enjoys discussing bodily functions? Sometimes this trait is referred to as biological rhythms. Understanding your child's regularity can teach you a lot about them. So, it's time to get a little gross. Children with high regularity are consistent with their biological functions. They often poop around the same time every day, get hungry at predictable times, and have a set sleep schedule (even if it is a schedule that their parents don't like). As they get older, they tend to be organized and enjoy consistent routines.

Children with low regularity have unpredictable biological functions. They may poop three times a day and then nothing for the next two days. They may fall asleep easily one night and take over an hour to fall asleep the next night. They may never be hungry for a full meal and prefer to graze instead. It's amazing how challenging this attribute may be.

It can be very frustrating to parent a child who does not eat dinner with the family at 6:00 p.m. and then complains about being hungry at 6:30 p.m. It can be irritating to have a child unexpectedly fall asleep in the car while you are driving home from work and then refuse to go to bed until 10:30 p.m. Understand that your child is not trying to make your life difficult by having regular or irregular biological functions.

Working with the degree of regularity that your child possesses will make your life a lot easier. Try not to make a quick run to the grocery store if it is around the time that your high-regularity child usually needs to nap. Consider having a flexible mealtime for your low-regularity child. Take a noise machine with you on vacation if your high-regularity child uses it nightly to help them sleep. Again, this is about working with the attributes your child has, not the ones you want them to have.

My son has high regularity, though he did not sleep through the night on a regular basis until he was five years old. I know what you are thinking. Huh? High regularity yet struggled with sleep for years? Yes, you read that correctly. Remember, regularity relates to consistency. My son awoke at predictable times each night and stayed awake for an amount of time that was consistent night after night. It was exhausting and frustrating, but it was predictable. I hated his sleep schedule, yet it was consistent and regular. These days, unless he is at a sleepover, he falls asleep within ten minutes of his bedtime. High regularity, as with all traits, can be disguised if we as parents do not take the time to put aside our expectations and perspectives.

I cannot explain how important it is to be objective when it comes to analyzing your child's attributes of temperament. I could have saved myself years of stress, worry, and agony if I had taken the time to understand attributes of temperament when my son was an infant. His sleep pattern was highly regular, it was just not a pattern that I liked or wanted.

Persistence

Before we dive into persistence, I need you to understand that persistence is not the same as resilience. These concepts are very, very different. Persistence is innate, and resilience is learned. A child with low persistence can be highly resilient. If you want to learn more about resilience, I highly recommend that you read *Building Resilience in Children and Teens: Giving Kids Roots and Wings* by Kenneth Ginsburg, MD.[1]

Children with high persistence will continue to attempt a task even if it is challenging. They are more likely to continue to practice something they want to master. Children with high persistence are likely to complete tasks independently. It's important for parents to check in with their high-persistence children to see if they need any help. Just because a child is working on a task alone does not mean that they are doing it correctly or safely.

On the other hand, children with low persistence tend to move on to a new task if the previous task was perceived as too challenging. These are the kids who have a hard time learning how to ride a bike or tie their shoes because they don't want to practice. They may even have a giant meltdown when trying to complete a task. If you are parenting a child with low persistence, you need to expect pushback when it comes to challenging situations. Resist the urge to label someone with low persistence as a "quitter." That does not help that person magically develop more persistence. Remember, a person with low persistence has not chosen this attribute.

Neither of my kids has high persistence, yet their dad has the highest level of persistence that I have ever seen. I love his tenacity, but it also creates conflict. You can imagine the challenges that occur in our home when it comes to learning something new. My husband wants our kids to keep trying until they master the skill in front of them. I frequently have to remind my husband that our kids are trying their best and that his level of persistence is off-the-charts high. He needs to gently be reminded to temper his expectations because those expectations are too high based on the temperamental traits of our children.

Mood

Children with a positive mood appear to be happy and optimistic. They are often cheerful and bubbly. Children with a negative mood appear subdued or even gloomy at times. This does not mean that children with a negative mood do not experience positive emotions or experiences, because they do! They just don't tend to show it externally. I personally do not like the term "negative mood." I prefer the term "serious mood" instead.

Goodness of fit tends to be particularly important when it comes to the attribute of mood. Parents with serious mood tend to be overwhelmed by the expressiveness of their kids who have a positive mood. Similarly, parents with positive mood tend to be disappointed when their serious mood kids do not demonstrate happiness or excitement. Understanding and acceptance are key.

Think about your child's most recent birthday party. Did they shriek with excitement over every gift they unwrapped? That's a child with a positive mood. Or did they open each present, thank the giver, and move on to the next without fanfare? That's a child with a serious mood. Again, neither positive mood or serious mood is inherently good or bad. You may need to explain your child's mood to friends and relatives. That's okay, just don't apologize for your child. Their mood is just their mood.

It's important to note that mood as a temperamental concept is not the same as mood as an affective concept. This distinction is incredibly important. Mood as a temperamental construct relates to the overall manner in which a person relates to the world around them, not to their internal affective state. Children with a positive temperamental mood are not immune to developing depression, anxiety, or other mental health disorders. Similarly, children with a serious mood are not destined to develop mental health disorders.

When it comes to temperament, mood relates to demonstration of happiness, joyfulness, and excitement. Children with a high mood demonstrate considerable excitement about life events. Children with a low mood may internally experience a high level of excitement, yet their external expression may be much more subtle.

My children, my husband, and I all have a positive mood. Birthday celebrations in our home are loud and full of energy. Sporting events are viewed with excitement and a lot of cheering or booing, depending on the circumstances unfolding on the television. That's not to say that we are always happy, cheerful people. Yet, chances are, if you visited our home, you would notice a lot of laughing and hugging.

I encourage you to take the time to identify your child's temperamental attributes, as well as your own. Apply this information to your parenting strategies. In the next chapter, I will help you do just that.

15

A Final Word on Temperament

We can learn so much about our children, ourselves, and the important people in our lives when it comes to temperament. Let's go through an important exercise.

At a minimum, you need a pen and a piece of paper. Now, I'm a little extra. If you need scented paper, colored pens or markers, or stickers for decoration, I get it. You do you. I want you to draw nine double-sided arrows on that piece of paper. Above each arrow, I want you to write one of the components of temperament. Make a mark on the arrow to where your child falls on the high-low continuum. High level is on the right side of the arrow, and low level is on the left side of the arrow. Take your time. Do this for each aspect of temperament, and for each child that you have. Then, repeat this exercise for yourself.

I don't have the words to explain how much this exercise will change your life. Again, understanding attributes of temperament can help you understand behavior, improve communication, and develop a stronger sense of empathy. Your relationships will deepen and become more impactful.

In fact, developing an awareness of temperament can help you in almost every single aspect of your daily life. It will help you understand why your best friend sobs loudly during romantic comedy movies. It can help you deal with an employee who you initially viewed as "lazy" because they move slowly. Understanding temperament can help you manage your interactions with Aunt Mary who consistently yells at your kids when she perceives them as being too loud.

I understand how overwhelming this may be. Please don't let that deter you. There is no time limit on this exercise. Take all the time that you need and make it fun! If this exercise seems daunting, don't worry about analyzing every single aspect of temperament all at once. Pick one or two aspects that are especially troubling and start with those. While you are analyzing attributes of temperament, please remind yourself that these features are innate. Judgment has no place here. Remind yourself to stay objective.

Once you have identified each trait of temperament for your child and for yourself, make a note if there is a goodness of fit. This aspect of the exercise may take some time. That's okay! There is no prize for getting to the temperament finish line first. Take the time to understand the temperament of everyone in your immediate family. Take the time to understand which aspects of temperament are causing conflict within your family. Utilize this knowledge to try to develop strategies to improve your parenting skills.

Let's go through an example:

The attribute is persistence. As I previously mentioned, my husband has an extremely high level of persistence. If there is something that he does not know how to do, he will watch YouTube videos until he understands the process. He insists on doing home improvements, even though he is a scientist with a PhD in nutritional biochemistry and no formal training in any trade. He has rewired parts of our home, installed vinyl plank flooring, removed and replaced trim, made and installed crown molding, installed drywall, replaced our pantry storage, and the list goes on.

My son, whose personality is so much like my husband's personality, has a moderate to low level of persistence. If he is not "good" at something, he doesn't want to do it. Everyday life happenings such as tying shoelaces and riding a bike took him a long time to learn, because he resisted practicing something challenging. When he was in fifth grade, Mason signed up for wrestling. In less than three full practices, he decided it was not a sport he wanted to continue. He assumed he wasn't good at it, and in turn, he didn't enjoy it. As a twelve-year-old, he would pull himself out of a baseball game if he felt his pitching was hurting his team.

My husband interpreted this as our son "quitting." He assumed that our son didn't try hard enough and that he didn't have the "drive" to persevere. He worried that this mentality would negatively affect our son for the rest of his life.

Yet, Mason loves football. He has never thrown in the towel and walked off the football field if he gets a penalty or if his team is not winning. My son's persistence is somewhat relative to the type of life experience, like most of us. Helping my husband understand my son's temperament strengthened their relationship and deepened the understanding that my husband has in regards to how our son relates to the world around him.

In fact, my husband was able to use this information to improve his parenting. As my son's coach, when Mason pulls himself from a baseball game, he no longer questions him. He substitutes him into a different position without a fuss.

There are certain things in life that we cannot avoid, no matter how low persistence may be. There are certain things we must learn, no matter how low approachability may be. There are certain things we must experience, no matter how high sensitivity may be. But understanding and working within the constructs of each attribute of temperament is how you can help your child thrive.

Understanding how your child's temperamental traits mesh (or don't mesh) with your temperamental traits can help you understand potential conflict and can help you to modify your parenting strategies. Utilizing the concepts of temperament and incorporating them into your parenting strategies will benefit both you and your child.

Let's switch gears a bit and explore how goodness of fit can shape our parenting strategies. Remember, goodness of fit relates to a person's temperamental compatibility with other people in their lives as well as the environment around them.

Goodness of Fit and Relationships

A child does not need to have the same degree of a temperamental trait to have goodness of fit with their parent. In fact, at times the opposite may be true. For example, a parent with a high activity level may benefit from having a child with a low activity level if they work multiple jobs and are exhausted at the end of the day. Likewise, a parent with low regularity may benefit from having a child with high regularity, who naps at predictable times each day.

Let's go through an example. A mom once brought her teenage daughter to see me because she was concerned that she was struggling with major depressive disorder. I'll call this teenager Delaney, which is not actually her real name. I had Delaney fill out a PHQ-9, which is a validated screening tool for depressive symptoms. Her score was low, indicating that she was not suffering from major depressive disorder. I asked Delaney how her mood usually was, and she replied, "Fine." I then asked her if she was depressed, and she said, "No."

At this point, Delaney's mom started to look frustrated. I asked her to explain her concerns. The mom said, "She just never seems happy. She doesn't get excited about things." I asked mom to think back to when Delaney was younger. "How did she act during her birthday parties, when people would sing her the Happy Birthday song?"

Mom responded, "She almost seemed embarrassed." I then asked mom to explain Delaney's behavior when she opened her birthday presents. Mom replied, "She was grateful for each gift, but never make a big deal about any of them."

Delaney was not suffering from major depressive disorder. Rather, the mom-daughter relationship lacked a goodness of fit when it came to the temperamental trait of mood. Mom had interpreted Delaney's negative mood as depression when it was anything but. I explained temperament, mood as a construct of temperament, and goodness of fit to Delaney and her mom. I gently told mom that while Delaney might feel big emotions, her behavioral response to those emotions would likely always be subdued. Delaney immediately looked relieved. My hope is that this discussion allowed mom to change her expectations when it came to Delaney's future behaviors.

Let's go through one more example, again from a patient in my medical practice. I once had the mom of a six-year-old, who I will call Ellie, bring her daughter in for concerns regarding ADHD. Prior to the visit, I asked mom and Ellie's teacher to complete Vanderbilt forms, which are validated assessments for ADHD symptoms. During the appointment, Ellie sat quietly and watched YouTube videos on her mom's phone. Mom expressed concerns that Ellie was "too active." She liked to run around and play. This was becoming problematic, because Ellie and her mom lived in a small apartment. Their downstairs neighbor frequently complained to their landlord about the noise that occurred while Ellie was playing.

I asked mom about Ellie's behavior at school. Mom reported that teachers never had anything but wonderful things to say about Ellie's behavior. She was a model student, and always sat and did her work. She was not disruptive, and she was well liked by her classmates.

To make a diagnosis of ADHD, you have to demonstrate a certain number of ADHD symptoms in at least two different environments. Ellie was not hyperactive at school. In fact, I doubt that she was hyperactive at home.

Ellie did not have ADHD; she simply had a high activity level. Unfortunately, there was a lack of goodness of fit between Ellie's environment and her activity level. Rather than trying to change Ellie's activity level, I was able to help mom identify strategies to manage this trait within her current home environment.

Taking the time to understand temperament, reflecting on goodness of fit, and applying this information to our parenting styles is absolutely worth the effort. This knowledge will deepen parent-child relationships and help set appropriate behavioral expectations. Furthermore, it can allow parents to help increase the goodness of fit in relationships and with the environment.

PART V

PARENTING POWER MOVES

16

Putting Development into Practice

There is a huge difference between understanding your child's development and putting that knowledge into practice. It's like learning how to ride a bike. You may understand the steps needed to balance, push the pedals, and move, yet there is a big difference between understanding and doing. If you want to develop a more effective and peaceful parenting journey that centers around the child you have, here are some universal tools to help you. They are conceptually simple, yet require practice to be effective.

Identify and Avoid Triggers

Whenever you are dealing with a behavior that you don't like, you need to understand that there are always triggers for that behavior. If you can anticipate and avoid those triggers, the problematic behaviors significantly decrease in frequency and intensity. Identify and avoid the triggers, and behavior improves. Common triggers for misbehavior are:

- Being tired
- Being hungry

- Being over-stimulated

- Being angry

In fact, these four triggers are almost universal, even for adults. Your child may have additional triggers, and I encourage you to spend some time thinking about those triggers. Write them down, if needed.

It is important to understand that avoiding triggers does not mean that you are somehow "giving in" to your child's demands. It is quite the opposite. For many parents, this is a concept that is challenging to understand. Most of us were raised with the mentality that children are supposed to acquiesce to their parents' demands. Our own parents most likely never gave a thought as to what triggered our childhood problematic behaviors. They simply punished us when we stepped out of line. There is a better way.

Avoiding triggers for unwanted behavior is based on a parent's understanding and accepting their child's individual qualities and current developmental abilities. This does not need to be a rigid concept; in fact, it is meant to be flexible and supportive. Recognizing and avoiding triggers is a child-centered approach that is very much aligned with the concept of parenting the child you have.

I encourage you to do your best to avoid your child's triggers for unwanted behaviors. Here are some suggestions. Take snacks with you everywhere you go. Bring toys or activities with you on outings to prevent your child from getting bored. If you are in an environment that is highly stimulating, consider bringing headphones or sunglasses for your child. Don't allow your teenager to stay up until midnight if they have to be at work at 6:30 a.m. the following day. Remember, if you actively ignore your child's triggers, you are setting them up to misbehave.

I once spoke with a mom who was excited about taking her children on an airplane for the first time. They were traveling to Florida and were very happy that they found cheap airfare. The only problem was that their children would have to wake up at 4:30 a.m. in order to arrive at the airport on time.

The parents tried everything to encourage their kids to go to bed early. However, the kids were so excited about the trip that they stayed up past their bedtime. Inevitably, the kids were exhausted and cranky the morning of their flight. Multiple meltdowns ensued, both at home and in the airport. People stared. A few "brave" people made disparaging comments to the parents. The first day of their trip was miserable, all because the parents ignored their child's triggers.

While avoiding triggers may decrease undesirable behaviors, talking about triggers for misbehavior enhances brain development. Identifying and discussing triggers can be a great learning opportunity for your child. The next time they act up because they are hungry, you can say, "Gosh, I get cranky too when I am hungry. Would you like a snack?" Or, "You seem really angry. If someone took my cookies, I would be angry too. Do you need to punch a pillow?"

It may seem silly, but identifying your child's physical and emotional states helps them to understand those states and to take ownership over them. Verbally addressing your child's physical and emotional states helps to create, and reinforce, desired synaptic pathways.

Identifying and avoiding triggers for misbehavior not only decreases the frequency and intensity of undesired behaviors, it also provides a learning opportunity for discussions about emotions and desired behaviors.

Find and Maintain Your Calm

Let's be honest. Sometimes our child's behavior pisses us off. However, you don't want to respond to that behavior in a way that encourages it to continue. That's why it is so important to stay calm. Take a few deep breaths and make sure to engage the frontal lobes of your brain before you respond to your child's undesired behavior.

I like to think of parenting responses to unwanted behavior in terms of zones. The most effective parenting zone is the green-light zone. This zone is calm and rational. In this zone, you are able to access your neocortex and think before you respond. You stay in control of your thoughts and actions. This will enable you to provide appropriate discipline that benefits your child.

The yellow-light zone is often ignored by most parents, because it takes a significant amount of self-awareness. This is the zone where physiological responses kick in—heart rate increases, breathing patterns quicken, alertness increases. The body is preparing for a fight. During this zone, the neocortex can still take over, but only if a parent recognizes that the emotional brain is preparing to make an appearance.

The red-light zone is on a power trip. It's angry and insistent on improved behavior, yet lacks the control to encourage improved behavior. Yelling, shaming, and spanking are red-light zone behaviors. They are expressions of the fight response of the amygdala. Red-light responses may create a desired outcome in the moment, but they are setting the stage for undesirable behavior in the future.

I have a mom in my medical practice who relies on yelling when her children misbehave. When her children were toddlers, this method controlled their unwanted behavior. Let me be honest. Her yelling scared the crap out of her children when they were young. You could see it in their faces, and at times they would physically shake in fear. She was aggressive and mean and scary.

As her children grew older, stronger, and bigger, they started to yell back at their mom. They would cuss at her and act aggressively. The aggressive behavior occurred at home and at school, and caused significant problems. There is no judgment here, but those children learned their aggressive behavior from their mom.

If you yell at your child, they will learn to yell. If you name-call your child, they will learn to name-call. At the same time, if you praise your child, they will learn to praise others. If you respect your child time and time again, they will learn to respect you and others. We explored this phenomenon previously in the chapter on modeling. For now, I encourage you to focus on efforts to get into your personal green-light zone.

In order to access the green-light zone, you have to tap into your amazing neocortex. You must demonstrate self-control and restraint even when every fiber of your being wants to throttle your child. Creating and maintaining a calm demeanor when dealing with your child's problematic behavior is essential. You need to take some time to explore and develop the calm within you, even in times when you feel like you are about to explode.

If this concept feels foreign to you, I encourage you to imagine yourself as a scientist. You are wearing a lab coat, have a beaker in your hand, and you are excited for knowledge. Each time you experience something new, uncomfortable, or unsettling, think to yourself, "Isn't that interesting? I wonder where that came from?"

This perspective is one of exploration and learning; this scientist mentality will help you evaluate your child's behavior without judgment. This type of mentality takes time, so please be patient with yourself. I promise you, if you can learn to observe your child's problematic behavior in an objective manner, you will be better equipped to respond to that behavior.

In my experience, the best way to encourage the appearance of the green-light zone is to adopt a mantra that you will use time and time again to remind yourself to calm down and think before you react to your child's behavior. For me, that mantra is "Duck on a Pond." I stole this phrase from my husband.

Years ago, when my husband and I were dating, we were at an airport when our flight was abruptly cancelled late in the evening. We had an important event to attend several states away, and the cancellation was unacceptable to me. I am not proud of this, but I proceeded to get into a heated discussion with the poor airline staff about options. I was rude and demanding, and I regret my immature behavior. Not surprisingly, despite my best efforts, I could not convince them to change their minds and un-cancel the flight. Apparently, you can't reason with bad weather.

I was sweating, my heart was racing, and I was irate. I looked over at my then-boyfriend, who was actually smiling. I demanded to know why in the face of this awful, horrible situation, he managed to smile. He simply said, "Duck on a pond, baby. I'm a duck on a pond." At the time, that made me even angrier. I stormed off toward the rental car, leaving him to carry our luggage.

It took years for me to truly understand what he meant.

I want you to picture a duck floating on the surface of a pond. It looks so calm and peaceful, and it glides across the water with effortless grace. Yet under the surface of the water, its little duck legs and webbed feet are kicking furiously in an effort to move forward. Under the water is chaos, but above the surface is serenity. Effective parenting means being a duck on a pond.

When my kids fight with each other or say hurtful things, I get mad! Sometimes I want to scream at them about their behavior. Yet I know that yelling at them will not bring about the behavior I would like them to demonstrate. Instead, I close my eyes, imagine a duck on a pond, and take a few deep breaths. This helps me to calm down and think about my actions before I react.

If your child does something naughty, it is normal to feel angry or disappointed or embarrassed. Your emotions are completely valid, but the actions you engage in as a response to those emotions may be detrimental to your parenting goals. Remember that your actions have consequences. Despite any strong feelings that you may have, you need to act like a duck on a pond.

I strongly encourage you to find a word, phrase, or visualization that helps you to calm down and become grounded before you respond to your child's misbehavior. "Duck on a pond" may not resonate with you, and that is okay! Finding your own calm-down, green-light-zone mantra may take some trial and error.

If you try a duck-on-a-pond phrase that does not suit you, please do not despair! It's part of the process. You may be able to use that image or phrase in other aspects of your life. Keep experimenting, and eventually, you will discover your green-light-zone phrase. This is your mantra.

Once you determine your mantra, you need to implement it. Your mantra will not be effective unless you use it multiple times a day. Write your mantra on a post-it note and stick it on your bathroom mirror or on your refrigerator if you need to. Talk to your partner and see if you can get them on board with this approach. Keep practicing and remind yourself that changing patterns of behavior takes time.

By utilizing a mantra to help you think before you react, you are creating a new pattern of behavior. You are actually modifying the synaptic pathways in your brain by practicing your mantra. Isn't the human brain incredible? In attempts to guide your child's brain development, you are actually developing new pathways in your own brain.

Remove the Phrase, "My parents did (insert behavior here) and I turned out okay" from Your Vocabulary.

The truth about this phrase is that it is intended to justify a behavior that a person inherently, and perhaps subconsciously, knows is detrimental. Let that sink in. This phrase is an excuse to stay stuck in the past, to perpetuate generational trauma, and to act like a jerk toward your kids. This phrase is a power trip in disguise, as well as a way to pretend that you are fine when you actually are not fine.

Please make yourself a promise to never let that phrase enter your consciousness in the future, at least without challenging this thought as absolute crap.

Let's go through an example. Theo is a three-year-old whose parents are frustrated because he has been hitting other kids at daycare. They are tired of receiving phone calls from the daycare teachers about Theo's aggressive behavior. Both parents admit that they have an "old-school" approach to parenting. They have been spanking Theo since he started misbehaving at twelve months of age. Spanking or being hit with a belt was the discipline approach that their parents took with them, and they turned out okay (or so they say). They use this excuse to justify the punishments they inflict on Theo.

Theo's parents frequently talk to him about the importance of not hitting other kids at daycare. They insist, on a regular basis, that Theo complies with their demands to stop hitting at daycare. Yet they continue to spank him when he misbehaves. After all, that is how their parents raised them. Not surprisingly, Theo became increasingly more aggressive at daycare. His hitting intensified, he started to break toys, bite his teachers, and threw chairs on a regular basis. Eventually, when Theo was about to be expelled from school, his parents enrolled in a parenting course.

Time for another example. This time, five-year-old Emma is the child of parents who dismiss emotional expression. Their mindset is, "My parents didn't ask about my emotions and I turned out okay." Emma's parents recently got divorced. Suddenly, her entire world is flipped upside down. She does not understand her new environment, and she begins to act out. She cries frequently and has numerous temper tantrums each day. Her parents are at their wits' end trying to deal with her problematic behavior. As a result, Emma is subjected to repeated punishments and faces daily criticism about her behavior, because her parents ignore anything related to Emma's emotional experience. If Emma's parents wanted her behavior to change, they would need to challenge their own beliefs about emotions and validate Emma's emotional experiences.

I cannot fathom how repeated beatings with a belt, encouragement of emotional suppression, or demands of complete obedience didn't traumatize anyone, much less led to them being okay. To me, when someone tells me that they turned out "okay," they usually didn't. They are either in denial or lack the ability to articulate their experience.

I want you to view this phrase as a cop-out. It's an excuse. And it will ultimately hurt your child. If you have ever used this phrase, I need you to take a journey into your past and figure out why. Then I need you to open yourself to the possibility that you are probably not "okay" because of the way you were treated. I understand that this is asking a lot from you. From a personal perspective, I have needed therapy to help me work through some of my presumed okay-ness issues.

Consider this: if you were actually "okay," you would not feel the need to express that okay-ness to someone else. Did you catch that? Someone who is actually "okay" does not have a need to defend their "okay-ness" to someone else. You would be at peace with it, and it would not come up in a conversation. Likewise, if something that you experienced in childhood was traumatic, you would not hide it. You may not flaunt it, but if the issue came up, you would discuss it objectively.

Do you remember when I mentioned that initially, new parents will parent in the same way their parents parented them, or they will fight like hell to parent their child in the exact opposite way, because they recognize that what their parents did was traumatizing? For the latter, they unconsciously recognize that in some respect, they did not turn out okay.

Please understand that there is no judgment here. I truly believe that the majority of parents do what they believe to be best until they are motivated to do better. Let me give you one final example. I used to have an acquaintance who was in the foster care system for a portion of her childhood. She had an incredibly difficult life as a child. As she was navigating life as a parent, I tried to be understanding and supportive. Yet, she frequently utilized yelling and intimidation in her approach to parenting her children. When I asked her about her approach, she told me, "My mom screamed at me, and I turned out okay."

It took an incredible amount of self-control for me to refrain from saying, "No, you did not turn out okay. You were traumatized, and that trauma is now being transferred to your children." Unfortunately, she failed to recognize the trauma. She frequently yelled at her children. She implemented consequences that were brutal and detrimental to her children's development.

If no one has ever encouraged you to objectively analyze how your parents' parenting methods affected you, I apologize. In order to plan where you are going, you need to understand your past. I want you to think about your parents' parenting strategies, and I want you to do this objectively. By reflecting on the strategies that were implemented during your childhood, you can break the generational cycles of trauma.

That's not to say that everyone experienced negative parenting. Far from it! There are plenty of examples of people who were raised under positive parenting strategies. I have a family in my medical practice who were able to teach their daughter a deep breathing exercise at a very young age. I was impressed when I saw this child utilize this exercise at eighteen months old to calm herself down before receiving immunizations.

In my experience, most people were raised with both positive and negative parenting strategies. Rather than dwell on the negative, I'd also like you to reflect on the strategies that your parents implemented that helped you to thrive. For example, when my mom was young, she was forced to eat everything on her plate. This was a common practice for people who survived the Great Depression. My mom hated it. When she became a parent, she was very intentional about letting my brother and me eat when we were hungry and stop when we were full. That was a huge parenting win.

I have an exercise for you to try. Adopt the scientist mentality of being objective and nonjudgmental. Take a piece of paper and divide the page into four sections. In the upper left section, I want you to write, "Parenting strategies that were negative." In the upper right section, I want you to write, "Parenting strategies that were positive." In the bottom left section, I want you to write, "How I will parent differently." In the bottom right section, I want you to write, "How I will parent similarly." As your children grow, you may want to repeat this exercise in the future.

There are many characteristics that I consider to be parenting superpowers. Avoiding triggers for misbehavior, being a duck on a pond, attempting to break the cycle of trauma, and recognizing the positive parenting our own parents employed are a few of them. In an upcoming chapter, we will explore another superpower, that of making mistakes. For now, we shift our focus to family meetings and mission statements.

17

Mission Statements and Family Meetings

At first, most parents raise their children in one of two ways—doing what their own parents did or doing the exact opposite of what their own parents did. If you grew up in a home where yelling was the norm, at first, you will either yell at your own kids or focus your efforts on not yelling at your kids. On the other hand, if you were raised in a home that valued hugs and other forms of physical affection, at first, you will either hug your children regularly or avoid physical contact. People will do what they know until they are motivated to change.

In the previous chapter, I highlighted the importance of reflecting on how your own parents chose to parent you. It's important to think about how you want to raise your child, and to do so on a regular basis. This concept may be foreign to you, and that is okay. Oftentimes, parenting is something that we do unconsciously. Has anyone ever "taught" you how to be an amazing parent? The answer is no (until now). Prenatal visits don't address successful parenting practices. Often, parents are not introduced to the concept of successful parenting until after their child is born. Even then, the vast amount of information about the "right" way to parent is overwhelming.

Think about how your life as a parent likely started. Once your baby was born, you were instantly sleep-deprived. You had this tiny, fragile human that became a twenty-four hour a day, seven-day a week responsibility. They relied on you for everything, yet could not communicate their wants or needs in a manner other than crying. In the early days of being a parent, it's normal to feel like you are in survival mode. That's okay!

Once you settle into your life as parent, it's important to bring your current and desired parenting styles into full awareness. This may be daunting because most of us have never been asked to analyze our parenting abilities. It may be a little uncomfortable, or a lot uncomfortable. Let's get uncomfortable. I want you to commit to being honest with yourself. You may uncover aspects of yourself that you don't like. It's okay. In order to become the parent, and the person, that you want to be, you need to understand where you are, right here and right now.

In life, one of the most important aspects of understanding ourselves relates to mindset. According to the *Merriam-Webster Dictionary*, "mindset" is defined as "a mental attitude or inclination." To me, mindset involves the way in which we think and believe. I challenge you to think about your current parenting abilities. Take some time and answer the following questions. Make sure to write these answers down.

- In what ways do I excel at parenting?
- In what ways would I like to improve?
- Overall, do I feel successful at parenting?
- Why or why not?
- How does a successful parent discipline their child?
- What factors make parenting my child rewarding?
- What factors make parenting my child challenging?

Take the time to sit with these answers. Resist the urge to judge yourself, especially if the answer is, "I don't know." Adopt that scientist mentality. You have already learned about your child's neurocognitive, emotional, and social development. You have determined your child's temperament. You have acquired so much knowledge in a short time. It is going to take some time to process that information and use it in a meaningful way. Give yourself some credit.

I have another exercise for you. I strongly encourage you to create a family mission statement. This term was developed by Stephen Covey and is defined as "A family mission statement is a combined, unified expression from all family members of what your family is all about—what it is you really want to do and be—and the principles you choose to govern your family life."[1]

In the corporate world, a mission statement is meant to explain a company's purpose for existing. It often includes information related to the company's values, culture, goals, and agenda. In addition to mission statements, many corporations also have vision statements. Vision statements are focused on future goals and achievements.

A family mission statement is a mash-up of a mission statement and a vision statement. It allows parents to focus on their parenting mission and to identify the goals that they have for their family. It also helps to guide future behaviors for everyone in the family. There is no right or wrong way to create a family mission statement. Likewise, there is no right or wrong information that is included in a family mission statement. Each statement is uniquely personal.

Within your family mission statement, you may want to address family values, discipline strategies, and/or characteristics of the home environment. Think of your family's positive attributes, the goals you have for each other, and the behaviors you would like to see in the future.

Creating a family mission statement may seem daunting at first. Remember, there is no right or wrong way to do this. However, involving the entire family in the creation of the family mission statement is important, even if your children are too young to provide input. You do not need to do this in one sitting. In fact, if you have young children, you may need to have several different get-togethers in order to create your family's mission statement.

During the family mission statement discussions, it's important to value everyone's input. It's okay if your young children offer silly suggestions, such as "let's include eating cheeseburgers every week in our family mission statement!" Make sure to take notes. Most importantly, have fun! This is not meant to be a chore. The intention is to help create unity, solidify values, and develop a principled home environment. I'd like to share my family's mission statement with you:

> In our home we value kindness, compassion, love, and respect. Open, honest communications about any topic will always be encouraged and allowed, and everyone's opinion will be valued. We will welcome and encourage the expression of emotions, thoughts, and beliefs. We will do our best to express ourselves in healthful, positive manners. When it comes to behavior, our focus is on effort rather than outcome. Discipline will never be based on fear or punishment, but rather on helping Mason and Savannah learn to make better choices in the future.

My goal as a mom is to raise kind, respectful, and caring kids who have all of the tools to follow their dreams and become successful adults who make the world a better place. Our family mission statement reflects that goal.

Take the time to create a family mission statement for your home. The impact can be immense. Your family mission statement may be very different from mine, and that is okay! As long as your mission statement includes your values, agenda, and intended culture, it is the best mission statement for you and your family. My only advice is that you do not make your mission statement too rigid. This is the exact reason that I included "try my best" in our mission statement.

A family mission statement is meant to help guide behavior. It helps provide structure and purpose within a family unit. It is not intended to be another "rule" for your children to follow. Similarly, the family mission statement is not meant to be exclusive to the children in the home. It's important that everyone in the family is held accountable to the family mission statement.

Let's go through an example using my family's mission statement. Imagine a situation where a child got into trouble at recess for fighting with another child. If the child's parent proceeds to berate the principal for attempting to correct the child's behavior, this is in direct conflict with the family's mission statement, which values kindness and respect. This creates confusion for the child and may lead to inconsistent parenting. If you are going to create a family mission statement, and I strongly encourage you to do so, you must act in accordance with that statement. Make sure to hold everyone in the family accountable as well, in a developmentally appropriate way.

No one is perfect! You are going to act in ways that deviate from your family mission statement from time to time—we all do! Your kids are going to make mistakes that deviate from your family mission statement. That's okay too! Just make sure to talk about it. The goal of creating a family mission statement is to help you focus on the type of household you want to create. It helps you to determine your goals as a parent. It helps you, and all of the members of your family, to focus on values that are important in your home. Family mission statements foster cohesiveness, connectedness, and serve to strengthen relationships.

Time to switch gears and discuss the concept of meetings. Anyone who works in the corporate world is familiar with meetings; they are pervasive in the workplace. Meetings provide an opportunity to develop a common purpose, generate ideas and plans, problem-solve, make decisions, and encourage initiative. Effective meetings promote open communication, provide attendees with important information, and create future goals. Meetings are just as important for families as they are for corporations.

I encourage all parents to have regular family meetings. The content of the meetings does not matter as much as the opportunity to communicate and connect with one another. Whenever there is a change in routine, expectations, or some type of logistical issue, a family meeting would be beneficial. Whenever a major life event happens or if a specific problem arises, family meetings can make a huge impact.

At the end of each school year, my husband and I sit down with our kids for a school-year review. We ask the kids what they liked and didn't like about the year. We ask them if there is anything that they would like to do differently during the next school year. We then talk about our family plans for the summer, both the day-to-day stuff and any vacations we may be going on. Finally, we have a discussion about the learning expectations over the summer.

We have our kids do several workbook pages of grade-related schoolwork over the summer. They do not like doing workbooks over the summer. AT. ALL. Our school-year review meeting allows us to compromise and incorporate our kids' preferences into their schedule. For example, they may have to do three workbook pages a day, but they may be able to choose the topics and time of the day that they complete those workbook pages. If they have a busy day at their summer camp, we may adjust our workbook expectations. Again, we work together as a family to make decisions. Yet, at the same time, the adults do not acquiesce in matters that are non-negotiable. My kids may have a say in when and how those workbook pages will be completed, but skipping the workbooks altogether is not an option.

During family meetings, it is important that everyone has an equal opportunity to speak and express their opinions. Everyone's input should be listened to and respected. Giving kids a voice helps them to develop self-esteem. It helps them to recognize that all people deserve to be listened to and given respect. Family meetings are also great for helping children learn conflict-resolution skills. Finally, family meetings encourage emotional expression, the capacity to compromise, and provide an opportunity to celebrate each other's accomplishments.

However, it is important that grown-ups determine the outcomes of the family meetings. Certainly, any input from children is welcomed and considered. Yet the parents need to be responsible for all decision-making. Furthermore, any decisions that are made should be explained to children in age and developmentally appropriate terms.

When it comes to family meetings, collaboration is key. It's also helpful to set some ground rules: no yelling, try not to interrupt someone else when they are talking, and absolutely no use of electronic devices during the meeting are examples. If you have a very communicative family, it may be helpful to have a specific object that someone holds when it is their time to speak. Your family's rules may be different, and that is okay. Make sure that everyone in the family agrees to these rules. Do what you need to do to make these meetings work for your unique family.

Kids younger than five years old may not be able to sit through an entire meeting; I would suggest that their participation be optional. I would also suggest that any family member be allowed to request a family meeting for any reason. It's optimal to give appropriate notice and to determine the best time for the meeting as a family.

Certain topics will require multiple family meetings. Divorce, significant illness, death of a loved one, and moving are some examples. These are events that are massively stressful. Oftentimes, a sole family meeting to address the topic is not enough to listen to all opinions and determine appropriate future actions. Younger kids will be unable to sustain their attention for lengthy meetings. Also, it's important to understand that some people need time to process difficult situations. Not all issues can be resolved in one sitting.

Time for an example. Let's say that dad has been offered a job out of state and the family is planning on moving. Before the move, it would be a good idea to have a family meeting. Dad can explain why this job is important to the family, what moving would entail, and when this move would happen. Then everyone in the family could express their thoughts and feelings about the possible move.

During this meeting, eight-year-old Ella immediately bursts into tears, cries, "I don't want to move!" then runs to her bedroom. The meeting is stopped, parents go comfort Ella, and they plan for an additional family meeting in the future. That's not to say that the family decides not to move simply because Ella had a meltdown. It just means that future discussions are needed. In fact, this family had several additional meetings about moving out of state. Ella was still sad, but she came to accept the decision to move.

There is no right or wrong way to have a family meeting, as long as everyone follows the predetermined meeting rules. There are, however, a few mistakes to avoid. At first, some family members may be resistant to family meetings. If the concept of a family meeting is new, give any reluctant family members some grace. It may take several conversations for them to understand the importance and benefits of participating in regular family meetings. Yet have the meetings anyway. Help children understand that while their input is valued, ultimately, the parents make the final decisions. Finally, don't lecture, argue, or get too far off-topic.

There is no best time of the day to have a family meeting. There is no ideal number of family meetings to have each week, month, or year. Some family meetings may be fairly short in duration, others will be longer. Sometimes the topic of the family meeting will be joyful and other times it may be more somber. The importance is that the opportunity for honest communication and connection exists. Family meetings are about coming together, checking in with each other, and working together to address problems, concerns, or challenging situations.

18

Understanding Common Parenting Misconceptions

In my experience, most parents want to do everything "right." This is especially true for first-time parents. But what does that even mean? It means that a person wants to be a super parent. They strive for perfection, despite the fact that perfection does not exist when it comes to parenting.

This is so important that I am going to write it again. There is no such thing as a perfect parent. Social media, pressure from friends and acquaintances, and our own internal experiences drive a desire to do everything right. Yet it's important to understand that super parents strive for unattainable goals.

These are the parents who want to sleep train their infant as soon as four months of age and expect them to consistently sleep through the night. They want a toddler who will eat vegetables on a regular basis. They want a child who never has a temper tantrum, especially not in public. Here's the truth. The desire to be a super parent is inherently based on the concept of parenting the child you want to have rather than the child that you actually have.

In fact, being a successful parent means getting uncomfortable with imperfection. It involves embracing mistakes. Instrumental to this process is analyzing several common parenting beliefs that are actually detrimental to a child's development.

I Need to Show My Child That I Am the Boss

Newsflash: Your child already knows that you are in charge, even if their behavior indicates otherwise. Trust this. Even if your child says, "You're not the boss of me!" or "I don't have to listen to you!" they don't actually want to be in charge. In fact, children crave consistency and security. They thrive when a parent is in charge.

You need to be the boss, yet it is important that you do not throw that boss-ness in your child's face. This is a delicate balance. It helps if you can view yourself as a leader to your child. I don't want you to be just any leader. In fact, when it comes to parenting, I want you to be a great leader. Great leaders have several qualities in common. Empathy, good communication skills, treating others with respect, and flexibility are a few. In addition, great leaders are confident and secure in their role. As a parent, you are in charge, and you have the final say in parenting and family decisions. Yet, rather than demand absolute compliance, it's important to stay humble and demonstrate integrity.

If you act like a know-it-all jerk who is always right, your child will grow up to resent you. If you insist that your child act subservient to your demands without explanation, you will not prepare your child for life in the real world. Rather, if you demonstrate consistency and exemplify confidence and compassion in your parenting strategies, you are a great parenting leader.

Great leaders are communicative and do not assume that others know what they are thinking. Please stop expecting your child to read your mind. They cannot and will not ever be able to read your mind. If you want them to do something, you will need to tell them so. If their actions are unwanted, you need to explain that to them. Finally, make sure to lead by example. Again, expecting a child to do as you say and not as you do will backfire.

It's important to create behavioral expectations and to set limits with your child. It's important to have honest discussions with your child about these expectations, and give them some choices when indicated. When conflict arises, validate your child's emotions, express your understanding of their requests, and respond appropriately. However, there is a way to assert calm, effective authority without shoving it into your child's face. At the same time, don't let your child become the alpha in the family. It's not cute when a child runs the show. We'll discuss this in more detail in an upcoming chapter.

If that sounds overwhelming, gently ask yourself if you are still trying to be a perfect parent. Oftentimes, when we become overwhelmed, it is because we need to reset our expectations. If you are not sure how to balance being in charge without being overly demanding or permissive, don't worry. That will be discussed soon.

For now, focus on your role as an authority figure. I promise, you can trust and believe that your child knows that you are the boss, as long as your actions support exactly that. Stop doing things and saying things to your children simply to demonstrate your power and your authority. Likewise, don't be wishy-washy and cater to your child's every whim, desire, and demand. Be consistent. More on that soon.

Crying Is a Sign of Weakness

Human beings experience emotions. Remember, there is not a single emotion that is inherently bad. All emotions are important and valid, and no feeling is final. The ways in which some people respond to their emotions may be negative or detrimental, but the emotion itself is not the problem.

Unfortunately, past generations have negated emotions. I have previously discussed how damaging this is. Never, ever demand your child to stop crying. Stop telling your child that their feelings are wrong, and do not tell them not to feel a certain way. In addition, refrain from telling your child that a certain experience is not scary. This is detrimental to their development.

Having a parent who is critical of a child's tears happens time and time again in my medical practice. Far too often, when a child cries because they are due to receive a vaccination, a parent barks, "Stop crying! It doesn't hurt!" In reality, receiving a vaccination is slightly uncomfortable, and many children are afraid of needles. Their fear is valid, and telling them that their emotions are wrong is, again, detrimental to their development.

Crying is a healthy expression of emotions, and it should not be discouraged. If you grew up believing that "big boys don't cry," or that you were supposed to suppress your emotions, I am so sorry that was your experience. Unfortunately, expression of emotions by crying is often considered shameful in our society, especially for males. I need you to change that mentality.

I want you to embrace the concept that crying is a healthy way to express emotions. There is no strength in repressing emotional expression. It's quite the opposite. Rather, I encourage you to view tears as a sign of strength and confidence. Tears indicate a person who is comfortable with emotional expression. At the same time, if your child's crying seems excessive, certainly reach out to your pediatrician. But please, don't try to suppress those tears or shame them out of existence. Be supportive. Be understanding.

My Child Should Be Doing XYZ because My Cousin's Friend's Son Started Doing XYZ a Month Ago

It is within our nature as human beings to compare ourselves to others. In 1954, psychologist Leon Festinger postulated that by comparing ourselves to others, we can evaluate ourselves.[1] These comparisons act as a benchmark. For example, if we attend a group exercise class, we may glance around the room to see how other participants adapt to the instructor's choreography. Comparisons can either be helpful and motivate a person to improve, or can be detrimental and lead to harmful behaviors such as cheating or stealing.

Within the parenting realm, comparisons are usually harmful. I never want a parent to compare their child to someone else's child (including siblings), or for a parent to compare themselves to another parent. When parents compare their child to another child, they end up being concerned that something is wrong with their child. They may project those fears onto their child, which only serves to diminish a child's self-esteem. When a parent compares themselves to another parent, they often feel less than.

Comparisons are problematic when we pick and choose certain aspects to compare, rather than looking at the whole picture. I have heard it time and time again in my medical practice. "Dr. Cook, my first child was running by twelve months of age. My youngest is thirteen months old and has not even taken a step!" Or, "All of my child's friends are in travel baseball, but honestly that is something we cannot afford. Does that make me a bad mom?" Or, "My sister has it all together. I'm such a mess compared to her."

Comparisons to others within the parenting realm will be problematic because they are made with incomplete information. No matter how close you are to a friend or family member, you do not know their entire story. You do not know what goes on in their home, behind closed doors. The information that people share with others is the information that they feel comfortable sharing. Similarly, it is easy to make assumptions about situations that we know little about.

Let's go through a quick example. You are in the grocery store one morning after being awake all night caring for a sick child. You are in sweats, without makeup, and your hair is in a mom-bun. You spot a mom in aisle five who is impeccably dressed, full face of makeup, and is wearing high heels while navigating two young, well-dressed children and a shopping cart. You think to yourself, "She's got it all together and I am a hot damn mess. My kids deserve better than me."

But unbeknownst to you, that mom is on her way to her dad's funeral. She realized that she didn't bring any food for her children on what was anticipated to be a long day, so she made a quick stop for snacks. Does that information make you reconsider your initial assessment?

I hope so. Every time you notice yourself making a comparison to other children or other parents, I want you to try to stop yourself. Remind yourself that you do not know the whole story. Acknowledge that a comparison made with incomplete information is inherently problematic. At the same time, do not feel any guilt or shame for making comparisons. Remember, comparisons are often a normal part of human nature. Yet, you may need to remind yourself that parenting comparisons do not serve your or your children. That's okay.

Let's go even deeper into the troublesome nature of comparisons. Possibly even more problematic than comparing yourself or your child to another human you know is the number of comparisons being made to complete strangers. This is rampant due to social media. How many times have you watched a video or read a post on social media, only to suddenly feel bad about yourself or your child? Social media can be problematic because each post is carefully curated. Pictures or videos that have been significantly altered, misinformation and even outright lies are able to be posted online. Each time you view something on social media, please remind yourself that the post may not even be remotely true. Be careful about the content that you are consuming on social media. That's not to say there is no valuable or authentic information on social media. There is. You just need to tread cautiously.

If you want to be the best parent that you can be, you need to become aware of your comparing behaviors. You need to recognize when you are comparing yourself to someone else, or when you are comparing your child to another child. Most importantly, you need to create an awareness that is devoid of judgment. Judging yourself fuels a cycle of feeling less than. Feeling less than will keep you stuck. Rather, assessing your experiences with an open mind and a desire to improve will put you on the path to success.

Are there other parenting "beliefs" that we need to question and analyze? Of course! Let's go through a few:

- I need to put my child first, even before my own needs.
- Parenting is something that comes naturally.
- I'm the adult, so I always know what is best.
- My child is not always happy, so I must be doing something wrong.

Remember, there is no such thing as a perfect parent. But there is such a thing as a self-aware, open-minded, and ever-evolving parent. Take some time to think about the misconceptions that may be affecting your parenting.

19

The Importance of Making Mistakes

In the previous chapter, I alluded to the mirage of being a super parent. Let's take it one step further. As a parent, you are going to make mistakes. In fact, you are going to make more mistakes than you can possibly count. Guess what? That's okay! In fact, by the end of this chapter, I hope that you view mistakes as a parenting superpower.

Despite all of my training and years of experience, I make parenting mistakes every single day. In fact, I make more than a few parenting mistakes on a daily basis. At times, I yell at my kids. Sometimes, I look at my phone while my child is trying to have a conversation with me. At times, I forget to order hot lunch for my kids or send them to school without gloves during the winter.

Mistakes are not bad. In reality, mistakes are an integral part of the human experience. Making mistakes is normal, common, and provides us with insight into valuable life lessons. Mistakes help us to grow and learn, which in turn helps us to encourage our children to grow and learn. I want you to invest in the importance of making mistakes and understand how mistakes actually make you a better parent.

Every parent yells. Every parent is at times more aggressive than they want to be. Every parent demonstrates impatience, gets frustrated with their child, and says something that they don't mean from time to time. No one is perfect; remember there is no such thing as a perfect parent. In fact, making mistakes helps you to break out of the construct of perfection.

Remember that scientific, nonjudgmental, and objective approach I discussed in earlier chapters? This can be very useful when it comes to the process of making mistakes. Whenever I make a mistake that causes harm to an adult, I go through a three-step process. I acknowledge the mistake, I apologize to the person who was harmed by my mistake, and I verbalize how I will try to avoid making the same mistake in the future.

Let's go through each of these steps in more detail. Acknowledging our mistakes fosters humility, self-compassion, and resiliency. Of course, these traits develop more fully if we avoid judgment and self-depreciation related to the mistake we made. It's important to separate the process of making mistakes from the concept of self-worth. You are not somehow a bad person because you made a mistake. At the same time, it's important to take responsibility for your actions. Getting defensive, blaming someone else, ignoring the mistake, and minimizing the consequences of that mistake are approaches that are detrimental to everyone involved.

After you acknowledge the mistake, make sure to apologize for it! The goal of an apology is to help someone feel empathy for others and to convey remorse for actions that caused harm. Try to be clear and concise. Apologies can help improve trust, provide validation, and enhance security by acknowledging that a hurtful behavior was unacceptable and won't be repeated.

But please make sure that the apology is sincere. Insincere apologies are obvious and do more harm than good. Insincere apologies can be distinguished by the time a person is seven years old. Insincere apologies may lack remorse, offer promises that will not be kept, or both.

Finally, briefly tell the other person how you will try to improve your actions in the future. Explain the actions you will take in attempts to not repeat the same mistake in the future. If you can acknowledge how a person seemed to feel after they experienced your mistake, that makes the apology even more powerful. Avoid the urge to make false promises. Again, sincerity is key.

This process is just as important when you make a mistake that involves your kids. Your kids will learn how to react to mistakes by watching your experience with mistakes. Anytime that I yell at my children, I apologize. Sometimes this happens immediately, other times it takes me a few minutes to calm down and think about my response. Regardless, anytime that one of my actions affects one of my kids in a negative manner, I always apologize. I know what you may be thinking. What, apologize to a child???

Yes! A mistake is a mistake, no matter how old the affected party is.

Let me give you an example. Let's say that you were late to drop your child off at their basketball practice. Their coach calls them out, they are embarrassed in front of their friends, and you issue an insincere, "Mommy is busy. So sorry." Your child feels invalidated, and your apology means nothing to them. If this happens on a regular basis, your child will learn that apologies are meaningless. If you want your child to apologize for their mistakes, you need to make sure that any apologies that you make are sincere.

Here's another example. Let's say that your child broke one of your favorite mugs. You yelled at him for being careless. You recognize that you yelled, and you tell your child, "I'm sorry I yelled, but you made Mommy so angry!" Yikes! Emotions are personal, and no one can make another human being feel anything. Please do not ever tell your child that they made you feel anything, because they didn't.

This may be a new concept for you. As a child, I frequently heard, "You made me so . . . [mad, sad, happy, insert emotion here]." Can you feel a certain emotion because of the actions of others? Sure. But again, emotions are created in our own psyche. Emotions are an internal experience, and often out of our control. However, the manner in which we behave as a result of those emotions is completely within our control.

Let's go back to the mug apology. Even if the parent is sincere, this apology is still problematic because it insinuates that the child was responsible for the behavior of the parent. Not only is this confusing for the child, but it is an excuse for a behavior that should not be excused. You need to own your emotions and your behaviors. If you acted out in anger, that's on you and not your child. A more appropriate apology would be, "I yelled because I felt sad because my favorite mug was broken. I am sorry that I yelled. If you try to be more careful, I will try really hard not to yell."

Did you catch that I said, "I will try really hard not to yell" instead of "Next time I won't yell"? The latter is more than likely a false promise, making the apology insincere.

When I make a mistake that involves my children, I expand my three-step approach to mistakes. Steps 1–3 are the same. I add step 4, which is asking my child if there is anything they would like to talk about. This reinforces the concept that mistakes are normal and provides my child the opportunity to ask questions. I encourage them to discuss their feelings. If they don't want to talk about it, I support their decision and ask them if there is anything that they need. Finally, in step 5, I ask my child if they would like a hug. If the answer is no, that's fine!

I approach apologies to my children with very intentional actions. I acknowledge, I apologize, I explain my intentions for future interactions, I offer the opportunity for discussion, and I ask if they need physical comfort.

Why is this important? Because it fosters security, emotional intelligence, and an understanding of, and an appreciation for, making amends. If you want your child to learn how to apologize for their indiscretions in a manner that is respectful, heartfelt, and meaningful, you need to make sure to apologize for your mistakes in the same manner.

You are not the only one who is going to make mistakes. Your kids will make a bunch of them. In fact, they will make more mistakes than you are able to count. It's important to hold your child accountable for their actions. The same rules apply. Do not make excuses for their mistakes. Do not blame others for their mistakes. Do not try to minimize the effect on the person who was hurt by your child's actions.

Because your child's brain is still developing, you may need to explain why their behavior warrants an apology. That's okay! There is a big difference between helping your child understand that what they did was wrong and ignoring the behavior because they may not understand the implications of their actions.

Remember that younger children are very egocentric, meaning they struggle to view the world from anyone's perspective other than their own. If they push another child who falls down and scrapes a knee, they aren't the ones who end up crying! It can be challenging for them to truly feel sorry for something they did not personally experience. Furthermore, it takes time for them to learn how to feel and express empathy.

Help your child to understand the physical, mental, and emotional experiences of the person who was hurt by their actions. Let's say that your child cut in front of their friend Billy on the playground. "Oh my, Billy is crying. I bet he is sad that instead of waiting your turn, you went to the front of the slide line. Do you remember how you felt when Riley wouldn't let you have a turn on the swing? How would you feel if someone took your place in line?" After explaining, it's a great idea to ask your child if they would like to apologize.

Finally, know that an apology is not the only way to express empathy and remorse. Other actions can take the place of an apology, especially for younger children. Rebuilding a block tower that was knocked over, replacing broken crayons, and including a child in a game they were previously left out of are all examples of making amends. This can be as meaningful, or more so, than saying, "I'm sorry." Even better, combine an apology with another behavior, such as helping to rebuild that tower.

While it's great to suggest that an apology is warranted, please don't ever force your child to apologize. If a child is not truly remorseful, forcing them to say "I'm sorry" is actually teaching them to lie. Please don't put your child in that situation.

In addition, forcing a child to apologize creates a power struggle. They may end up apologizing, but only do so to avoid punishment. Over time, that child will struggle to spontaneously apologize, as the thought of apologizing is associated with a loss of power.

In fact, when I was young, I was often encouraged to apologize for something that upset my mom, even if it was not my fault. My mom worked late on Thursday nights and often came home upset due to something that happened at work. Notably, whatever she was upset about had nothing to do with me, yet it was somehow still my fault. As a result, my dad encouraged (okay, nearly demanded) that I write my mom an apology letter for my perceived transgressions. I remember an apology letter I wrote to my mom when I was nine years old, which included the phrase, "I would never forgive myself if something bad happened to you." In my world, the grown-up was always right. Kid wrong, grown-up right. No matter what. You may have had a similar experience.

Some parents assume that they are always right, or that they know best, because they are the adult. They tell children, "Because I said so," instead of explaining the desired behavior or outcome. Such attitudes indicate that a parent values dominance and control at all costs and negates the concept of viewing mistakes as opportunities for learning and growth. I want you to pull out your family mission statement. If it includes terminology such as, "my children will obey me" or, "my family will respect my opinions above their own," you are in trouble. Not to mince words, but your kids will grow up to resent you. Being a successful parent involves collaboration and flexibility.

If you grew up in a home where the parent was always right, it may be challenging to view your behavior as a mistake. If you are not sure if your behavior warrants an apology, consider this: Did your behavior hurt or insult someone else? Did you behave in a manner that was hurtful or unfair? Did you fail to keep a promise? These are all mistakes that warrant an apology.

When I grew up, I promised myself that I would never force my child to make an apology. I would never demand that my child write an apology letter for something that was not their fault. I want my children to be remorseful for actions that hurt others, even if the intention was good. Apologizing is much more sincere if it is a desired behavior rather than something that is coerced.

It takes a strong person to be an authority figure who is honest and vulnerable. Own your messes, and your children will learn to own theirs. I have apologized to my children more times than I can count.

If you screw up, own up to it, apologize, and briefly explain how you are going to try to do better in the future. Then let it go. This may feel uncomfortable. It is probably going to take time and effort. But acknowledging and apologizing for your mistakes is such a powerful parenting tool. It is worth the effort.

In addition, this approach absolutely encourages more positive behavior from your child. Remember, your kids are constantly watching you and learning from your behavior. If you normalize mistakes and focus on learning from those mistakes, your kids will eventually do the same. It can be hard to admit that we did something wrong! Do it anyway. And then discuss how you would do things differently if you had that chance.

If you are still hesitant to welcome mistakes in your home, I have one question for you. Why? Mistakes are a part of life. We grow through experiencing challenges. Mistakes become learning opportunities when they are embraced and evaluated, instead of being dismissed. Again, own your mistakes, talk to your children about your mistakes in developmentally appropriate terms, and discuss how you plan to do better in the future. Then encourage your children to approach their own mistakes in the same manner.

PART VI

DISCIPLINE

20

Understanding Discipline

Being a parent means raising your child or children from infancy until adulthood. It involves supporting the neurocognitive, social, emotional, physical, and possibly spiritual development of that child or children. Simply put, parenting is the act of being a parent. It's important to understand a few terms when it comes to parenting. The first is discipline. Disciplining a child involves using certain styles and strategies in order to teach your child safe, appropriate behavior, as well as attempting to prevent behavioral problems. If behavioral problems occur, you as a parent consistently apply age and developmentally appropriate consequences.

The ultimate goal of discipline is to help your child gain the skills that they need to be responsible and successful adults. Discipline is about teaching. This is so important that I am going to write it in a slightly different way. Discipline involves instruction—helping kids to understand, in developmentally appropriate terms, as to why a certain behavior was desired or undesired and how they can act appropriately in the future.

Discipline is not the same thing as punishment—far from it. Rather than instructing, punishment involves inflicting pain or suffering as retribution for a negative action (such as a problematic behavior). Take the term "spare the rod, spoil the child." This biblical phrase is commonly misinterpreted as justification for using physical punishment, such as spanking. Yet numerous studies have demonstrated that punishment used to inflict physical pain causes increased aggression, mental health problems, and antisocial behavior.[1,2] Spanking, grounding, and time-outs that are incorrectly implemented are all examples of punishments. More on time-outs later.

More often than not, punishing is a power trip for the person inflicting the punishment. This power trip may be intentional (such as with spanking) or unintentional (usually the case with time-outs). Punishing is parent-focused while discipline is child-focused. Are there times when punishment is appropriate? Of course. If your child is about to stick a fork into an electrical outlet, you may need to smack their hand in order to prevent them from getting hurt. However, punishments should be used sparingly with young children.

As a child grows older, punishments in the form of taking away privileges may be an effective supplement to discipline. If you adopt this approach, you need to understand how important that privilege is to your child. If your child doesn't like playing video games, it makes no sense to unplug the PlayStation if they misbehave. However, if the privilege is desired by your child, you will be more effective if you offer your child the opportunity to earn the privilege back. For example, if you take your child's phone away because their room is a disaster, offer to give the phone back once the room is cleaned, and make sure to explain why having a clean room is important.

The most successful parents focus on discipline. They strive to educate their child or children. Any consequences that are provided for problematic behavior are intentional and well thought-out. Those consequences are given in order for a child to learn how to behave more appropriately in the future. On the other hand, punishment is about control and power. Punishments are rarely informative or educational. Effective discipline will almost always lead to the desired outcome in the long term much more than punishment will. Let me give you an example:

I had a parent of a two-year-old patient of mine express concerns about her child's behavior. Let's call this child Ariana. Ariana had recently started demonstrating aggressive behavior. She was hitting and biting. However, the most distressing aspect of this behavior, according to her mom, was that Ariana recently started laughing when her mom "popped her." Apparently, this mom had been using spanking and smacking as a punishment since the child was less than a year old. Mom was at a loss how to stop Ariana's hitting and biting, because her strategy of using physical punishment was no longer working.

Several aspects of parenting come into play with this scenario. Remember the concept of modeling? Every time that mom "popped" (i.e., hit) Ariana in response to an undesired behavior, she was teaching Ariana that hitting is an acceptable way to express displeasure with someone else. Remember, young children have no capacity to be rational. They cannot witness the behavior of others and interpret it to be inappropriate. They will act in the same manner as their caregivers are acting.

Ariana's laughing was a response to the power struggle that her mom had created by using punishment rather than discipline. Ariana was trying to regain some control. As a toddler, she craved autonomy. She was also likely trying to express an unmet need, probably an emotional need. Finally, no one taught Ariana how to behave more appropriately in the future. Remember, the developing human brain needs to know what to do; it is not helpful to tell someone what not to do.

Attempting to stop an unwanted behavior is far different from teaching a child to continue a desired behavior. If mom would have stopped "popping" Ariana, immediately addressed any aggressive behavior she displayed, and discussed with her in developmentally appropriate terms how to behave in a more productive manner, the aggressive behavior would have decreased dramatically.

As a parent, it is not your job to control your child's behavior. Attempts to do so will be counterproductive. Rather, your kids need you to teach them how to behave, through your words and through your actions. Successful discipline involves being responsive to a child's emotions and needs, setting consistent and appropriate limits, and at the same time, expecting a developmentally appropriate level of maturity from your child.

One of the most important aspects of successful discipline relates to consistency. Consistency involves acting in the same manner over and over again. This leads to predictable actions, behaviors, and responses. Consistency is an important aspect of daily schedules, routines, rules, expectations, and discipline. Being consistent in your parenting approach is a conscious choice that requires intentional engagement with your child.

Consistency has numerous benefits for neurocognitive, social, and emotional development. Repetitive experiences strengthen synaptic connections. The stronger the synaptic connection, the less likely that connection is to be pruned as the brain develops. In addition, consistency helps a child feel more comfortable exploring the world around them.

Consistent Schedules and Routines

Consistent routines are activities that occur at approximately the same time and happen in the same way from day to day. Getting into pajamas, followed by brushing teeth, going to the bathroom, climbing into bed, and having dad read two books is an example of a consistent bedtime routine. Consistent routines help a child to feel secure and safe; they help a child learn that their caregivers are trustworthy and reliable. The predictability associated with consistent routines also helps to encourage the development of independent behavior.

For example, if you make it a routine to put a toddler's coat on near the garage door before you leave for daycare, your child is more likely to learn that they need to put their coat on, and do so without reminders, before they go to elementary school. Instead, if you are inconsistent and sometimes put the coat on in the house, other times in the garage, and yet other times when they arrive at daycare, it will take your child longer to learn to put that coat on independently.

Consistency of routines will help your child understand and comply with behavioral expectations. If your child's bedtime is 8:00 p.m. night after night, they will be less inclined to fight going to bed. Let's be real. For most kids, bedtime is boring and will usually be met with some resistance. However, if you are inconsistent and one night you allow your child to stay up until 9:20 p.m., and another night allow them to stay up to 8:45 p.m., their level of bedtime resistance will be much higher. Consistency will set clear behavioral expectations, which is more likely to lead to compliance.

Does being consistent mean that you have to adhere to a strict time schedule every single day? Nope. Children who have a bedtime of 8:30 p.m. Sunday through Thursday and a bedtime of 9:15 p.m. on Fridays and Saturdays also have a consistent schedule. You may need to have several discussions about the reason for the different bedtimes to help set behavioral expectations.

Are you able to schedule your child's day down to the minute, every single day? Of course not! That would be ridiculous. Schedules and routines are not supposed to be completely rigid. Life happens, and schedules become disrupted. In many cases, life events are more important than maintaining a strict schedule. For example, if grandparents from out of state come to visit only once a year, let the kids stay up late in order to make the most out of that visit. That's okay! Make sure that you talk to your child about upcoming changes to their routine. Whenever possible, give them time to adjust to the changes.

However, if there are other caregivers in your child's day-to-day life, please make sure that they are aware of your child's routine. If grandma wants to watch your child for the day, make sure to discuss the importance of putting him down for a nap at his normal nap time, instead of keeping him awake because grandma is having fun playing with him. If you are like me, you may need to explain to grandma why it is not okay for her to let your four-year-old have sips of her beloved Pepsi instead of milk for lunch.

Consistency of routines is not supposed to be all-or-none. It's important to leave some wiggle room for special circumstances. The importance is in the overall patterns of behavior. In my experience, if you can provide a consistent routine for your child 85 percent of the time, their overall experience will be one of consistency.

Consistent Expectations

Consistent expectations are crucial to successful parenting. You need to set age-appropriate and developmentally appropriate behavioral expectations for your child. You need to make every effort to get everyone who is a caregiver to your child to adhere to the same expectations. Those expectations must be maintained as much as possible, no matter the external circumstances. As a parent, you need to put your money where your mouth is, no matter how tired, stressed, or overworked you may be.

Allowing a child to do something one day, then admonishing them for that same action the following day leads to confusion. This inconsistency, especially if it is a common occurrence, teaches a child that their parent is unpredictable and unreliable. Inconsistent expectations teach a child that their parent cannot be trusted. Please note that this does not apply to a one-time occurrence. Rather, it relates to a pattern of behavior over time.

Let's go through an example. You are the parent of an eight-year-old who is expected to read twenty minutes per day on school days. Yet sometimes, meeting this expectation is a challenge, because life happens. You pick up your child from their aftercare program at 5:00 p.m., race home for a quick dinner, then take him to a karate class at 6:00 p.m. You return home by 7:30 p.m., and it's time for reading. Your child would rather be on an electronic device and throws a fit about reading.

You have a choice. You can succumb to your child's demanding behavior, ignore the reading assignment, and take the easy way out. This will inevitably backfire, because it will teach your child that enough resistance results in them getting their way. This will lead to future pushback and misbehavior. The other option is to dig your heels in, maintain expectations, and figure out a way to get your child to complete their assignment. It may be helpful to apply discipline for misbehavior, which is the next focus.

Does committing to consistency mean that your child will never challenge you? Or that they will behave wonderfully all of the time? Of course not! But it will make your parenting journey a lot easier. Again, it's about trying to strike a balance. If you are consistent with routines, expectations, limit-setting, and providing consequences for misbehavior at least 80 to 85 percent of the time, congratulations. In my opinion, this means that you have achieved consistency.

21

Effective Discipline

Effective discipline is an incredibly complex subject. I'll try to keep it simple. To me, effective discipline involves teaching children how to act in kind, respectful, and socially appropriate ways. It's about setting the stage for successful and positive behavior and praising those positive behaviors when they occur. If a child misbehaves, the goal is to teach them how to do better in the future by providing age and developmentally appropriate consequences. Mistakes or shortcomings are acknowledged without judgment for the purpose of learning.

Effective discipline focuses on the behavior itself. It is very important to separate the behavior from the person and to verbalize that difference to our children. Doing something wrong does not mean that the person is wrong. Just because a child misbehaves does not mean that they are bad. Bad behavior is very different from a bad kid. Please, do not ever call your child a "bad girl" or "bad boy" when they misbehave. Rather, it's important to focus on the distinction between self and behavior.

As a parent with a fully developed brain, we understand this concept clearly. Our children, not so much. It's important to intentionally verbalize the difference. A child without a fully developed brain may automatically assume that they are wrong if they engage in an unwanted behavior, unless an adult tells them otherwise. As parents, we need to make sure that our responses to problematic behavior remain focused on the actual behavior.

Effective discipline involves providing consequences for undesired behaviors. Providing consequences for a child's misbehavior is twofold. The first aspect involves providing age and developmentally appropriate consequences that are in line with the degree of misbehavior. The second aspect involves consistently following through on the application of those consequences. This is often easier said than done.

It's possible that a certain behavior is best managed by ignoring and redirecting. This tends to be the case for many problematic behaviors that toddlers engage in. For example, if a toddler who is building a tower of blocks suddenly starts throwing the blocks across the room, it may be beneficial to ignore the throwing and instead say, "Oh look! I have a new book that we can read together!" This approach will cause the toddler to lose interest in the blocks and gravitate toward the novelty of the book.

Other undesired behaviors may be best managed by asking a child how they would respond if that behavior affected them. For example, if your son hits your daughter, you may want to calmly ask, "How would you feel if your sister hit you?" It may be helpful to suggest several possible emotional responses. Finally, it's possible that the best discipline strategy for a particular behavior is a natural consequence.

I love natural consequences! Natural consequences involve a direct cause and effect relationship that does not involve outside influences. In the case of natural consequences, the world provides the teaching, which means that you are off the hook! Let me give you an example. When my daughter was in preschool, one winter day she decided that she did not want to wear her coat to school. Instead of fighting with her or trying to force her into her winter coat, I calmly said, "Okay, but it's pretty cold outside today."

It was below freezing with the wind chill when we arrived at her preschool. She had a long sleeve tee-shirt and leggings on. I purposefully parked a few spots away from the front door. When we got inside, she exclaimed "Ooo, it's so cold!" And I said, "Yes, it's cold. It wouldn't have felt so cold if you had put on your winter coat like

Mommy asked." We didn't have another coat-related issue for the rest of the season.

Before you think, "Gosh, that's so mean!" please understand that I would never put my child in danger. It was cold, but it was not dangerously cold. At the time, there was not a more effective consequence that I as a parent could implement. Natural consequences can be amazingly successful as a discipline strategy, especially if a parent explains how a child can avoid that natural consequence in the future.

I have one caveat: never manipulate a natural consequence in order to turn it into a punishment. If I had forced my daughter to play outside on the school playground in the freezing cold for thirty minutes before allowing her to put on her coat, that is not a natural consequence. It's a punishment.

Let's go through another example of a natural consequence. Your teenager forgets to do their homework. As a parent, you can empathize with your child. But please do not finish that assignment for them. The inherent consequence is having to tell the teacher why the assignment was not completed and possibly getting a grade of zero. That teenager is best served by owning the mistake, telling their teacher the truth, and accepting the consequence of their actions without the involvement of a parent.

Think about the adult world. If an adult fails to fill their car's gas tank, the car will run out of gas and stop working, potentially leaving them stranded. If an adult fails to complete an important work assignment, they could be fired from their job. If an adult chooses to not pay child support, their wages could be garnished.

If a natural consequence is not available or desired, please be mindful that the consequence you give your child fits the severity of the misbehavior. If a child accidentally forgets to take out the trash, it is a little excessive to have them write a three-page essay on the importance of doing chores. Similarly, if a child pushes their friend to the ground at recess, giving them a hug and asking them to try harder in the future is a cop-out.

A consequence for an unwanted behavior will be more effective if it includes information about how the child could act in a more positive manner in the future. For example, if a four-year-old steals a cookie, you may want to ask for the cookie back and gently tell them, "It seems like you might have been hungry. If you want a treat, please ask me first." Or if a twelve-year-old fails to complete their chores, you may want to take away their phone and say, "It's important for you to learn about responsibility. You can earn your phone back once you have emptied the dishwasher."

Developing age and developmentally appropriate consequences for unwanted behaviors is really hard. As a parent, you need to temper your emotional brain, attempt to view the world from your child's perspective, then analyze the behavior in question in an objective manner before providing discipline for that behavior. It requires intention and a hell of a lot of practice. Be patient with yourself. I suggest a four-step process:

1. Acknowledge your child's emotional experience.
2. Briefly explain why the behavior was undesired.
3. Introduce your child to a consequence for misbehavior.
4. Discuss how your child could behave in a more appropriate manner in the future.

It's important to note that these steps do not need to be applied in order.

Let's go through a few examples. Imagine that you are a parent to a seven-year-old named Sam. Sam pushed his friend off of the swing at recess and had to go to the principal's office. You listen to the principal's account of the situation, as well as Sam's account. When you get home, you have a brief discussion with Sam. You tell him, "I understand that you became angry when your friend took the swing you wanted to use. However, pushing anyone is never okay. Because you pushed your friend, tomorrow you will have to stay indoors for recess. In the future, if there is a problem during recess, please talk about it with the recess attendant."

Now imagine that you are the parent to sixteen-year-old Sydney. Sydney chose to ride in a car her friend was driving, without a seatbelt.

Unfortunately, the car got into an accident, and she sustained a concussion. Once Sydney has received appropriate medical attention and you determine that she is okay, you have a brief discussion about her actions. You tell Sydney, "I cannot imagine how scared you must have felt during the accident. I am sorry that your head hurts, but I hope you understand how important it is to wear a seatbelt in the future." In this situation, the natural consequence that occurred has provided the majority of the teaching, which means that you can skip a few steps.

Let's switch gears and focus on the importance of implementing said consequences. The parenting fortune is in the follow-through. You have to put your money where your mouth is. If you have determined that a child needs a consequence for an unwanted behavior, you absolutely must follow through and administer that consequence. Effective discipline requires consistency. Otherwise, your child will perceive your inconsistency as untrustworthy and unpredictable. In turn, this will make them more likely to disobey you in the future.

When my son was young, my mom used to babysit him two times per week. My son is smart and strong-willed. That is a challenging combination in the younger years. One day when I was at my wit's end with his behavior, I said, "If you don't stop hitting, I will call GaGa and tell her not to come over tomorrow." GaGa is my mom; my son gifted her with this nickname, and it stuck. My proposed consequence for my son's problematic behavior was to tell my much-needed babysitter not to come over to watch my child when I needed to be at work.

Talk about a parenting fail. There is no way that I would actually follow through on that threatened consequence; I needed a babysitter! I let my emotional, reactive brain take over. As soon as the words came out of my mouth, I regretted them.

Do not ever threaten with a consequence that you know you will not be able to actually enforce. Ever. It does not even matter what that consequence is. Don't let the words even come out of your mouth. Don't bring it into existence. I cannot stress how important this is. You need to maintain your credibility as a parent who is consistent. Focus on the consequences that you will be able to enforce.

Enforcing age- and developmentally appropriate consequences that are congruent with the severity of the offense is an art. While the four-step process I previously introduced can be incredibly helpful, it only applies when punishments are avoided, the severity of the consequence matches the severity of the misbehavior, and when the behavior is assessed within the context of age- and developmental abilities.

For the purpose of this chapter, *punishments* are punitive and, in the majority of situations, should be avoided if they do not provide learning opportunities. *Age-inappropriate* means that the discipline strategy is beyond the child's current developmental abilities. *Incongruent severity* means that a punishment is out of proportion to the actual behavior. And finally, *age-appropriate* is an example of an effective and positive disciplinary strategy.

The first example is Charlie, a four-year-old girl who hit her mom because mom would not give her a cookie.

- Punishment: mom hits Charlie back to "show" her how much hitting hurts.
- Age-inappropriate: mom demands to know why Charlie hit her.
- Incongruent severity: mom completely ignores Charlie for the next two hours.
- Age-appropriate: mom immediately says, "Oww! Hitting hurts. Please don't hit. It's okay to be angry or frustrated. It's not okay to hit. Ask me for help instead."

The second example involves Jake, a ten-year-old boy who left his unfinished homework at school.

- Punishment: parent says, "Give me your phone. You lost it for the rest of the night."
- Age-inappropriate: parent says, "I want you to write me a five-page essay about the importance of doing homework and turning it in on time. Make sure to cite your sources."

- Incongruent severity: parent says, "Give me your phone. You lost it for the next 3 months. Don't you ever leave your homework at school again."
- Age-appropriate: parent says, "I would be upset if I left my homework at school. Yet mistakes happen. Do you think that you can email your teacher about the situation and do the homework tomorrow?"

The final example involves Brayden, a fifteen-year-old boy who came home ten minutes after his curfew.

- Punishment: parent says, "You are grounded for a week."
- Age-inappropriate response: parent says, "You'll never succeed in life if you cannot pay attention to the time. Tell me why punctuality is important."
- Incongruent severity: parent says, "You are grounded for two months."
- Age-appropriate: parent says, "It's late. I'm disappointed that you missed your curfew, but I bet you have a reasonable explanation. Please go to bed. Let's talk about why you missed your curfew in the morning, and what our next steps are."

Effective discipline involves implementing clear expectations for behavior. If problematic behavior arises, it is dealt with in a way that is age and developmentally appropriate. Consequences for problematic behavior are developed thoughtfully and implemented immediately. The severity of the consequence is in line with the actual offense. The consequence is something that a parent is absolutely able to implement. Finally, the goal of implementing the consequence is to help encourage the child to make better choices in the future.

If that sounds like a tall order, it is! Again, effective parenting is an art. It is not something that a person magically knows how to do once they bring a child into this world. It requires time, patience, and a commitment to learning and growing. Expect to make mistakes! Do the best you can do and never stop learning.

PART VII

PARENTING

The Struggle Is Real

22

Baumrind's Parenting Styles

Did you know that there are different styles of parenting? These are patterns of attitudes, behaviors, and approaches to parenting. Two of the most important aspects of parenting styles involve the concepts of responsiveness and demandingness.

"Responsiveness" refers to how much or how little a parent responds to their child's physical, social, and emotional needs. For example, if an infant cries, does a parent attempt to figure out what that baby needs and then meets that need in a timely manner? If a teenager breaks up with her boyfriend, does a parent recognize and validate the importance of that relationship? Or is it dismissed as "puppy love"?

"Demandingness" refers to how much a parent expects responsible and mature behavior from a child. For example, does a school-age child have age-appropriate chores to complete? Is a teenager expected to be home at a designated curfew?

Honestly, I don't love the term "demandingness." It feels a little harsh and bossy to me. I would have called it "expectedness." My caveat to demandingness is that it needs to account for developmentally appropriate behavior—which is why demandingness does not apply to infants and applies in a limited manner to toddlers.

Psychologists Diana Baumrind as well as Maccoby and Martin developed a theory involving four different parenting styles.[1] Each of these parenting styles involves a low or high level of responsiveness and a low or high level of demandingness. While many parents fall into one of these categories the majority of the time, please note that they can exist on a continuum. These parenting styles are categorized as authoritative, authoritarian, permissive, and neglectful.

Why does this information even matter? Because the way in which a person behaves toward their child or children will impact those kids for the rest of their lives. The degree of responsiveness and demandingness that a parent demonstrates affects a child's self-esteem, academic achievements, relationships with others, and even their mental health.

Authoritative Parenting

One of Baumrind's parenting styles is called authoritative. This parenting style involves high responsiveness and high demandingness. An authoritative parent is warm and affectionate, yet has expectations for developmentally appropriate behavior. An authoritative parent expresses clear consequences for behavior that is deemed unacceptable and follows through on implementing those consequences.

An authoritative parent is sensitive and responsive to their child's individual temperament and emotional needs. They utilize open discussions and explain the reason behind any rules; all discussions involve listening and responding to their child instead of speaking over them. An authoritative parent is able to validate a child's feelings while simultaneously demonstrating that the parent is in charge, without demanding that the child acknowledge that their parent is the boss of them.

Authoritative is considered to be the preferred parenting style, because it leads to improved outcomes as older children and adults. Children of authoritative parents have been shown to have higher academic achievements and tend to be more independent than children whose parents have adopted other parenting styles.[2] In addition, children of authoritative parents are more likely to develop secure attachments (remember this concept from previous chapters?).[3] They often develop strong self-esteem and have good social skills.

Here's an example of authoritative parenting. Let's say that parents receive a phone call from the school principal that their child received an in-school suspension for fighting. They are upset, but listen carefully to everything that the principal has to say. When their child gets home from school, they listen carefully to everything that their child has to say about the situation. Despite any strong feelings that they may have, the parents support their child's emotional needs.

They make statements such as "I understand how that may have caused you to feel angry," and "I can see why you did that." At the same time, authoritative parents hold the child accountable for their actions. They provide age-appropriate consequences that are consistent with the family's values. As a result, the child learns from the situation and understands how to act differently in the future.

Authoritative parenting cliff notes: high responsiveness and high demandingness. Tends to lead to better outcomes for a child.

Authoritarian Parenting

A second parenting style is called authoritarian. Parents who are authoritarian have low responsiveness and high demandingness. These parents adopt a "my way or the highway" mentality. This translates into one-way communication. Attempts to have discussions with, or disagree with, authoritative parents are interpreted as back talk. It's important to note that the child is not actually engaging in back talk, yet the parent perceives anything other than blind obedience as just that.

Authoritative parents have high expectations for their children's behavior, which usually involves absolute compliance with parental rules and regulations. Authoritative parents create rules and enforce consequences with little regard for their child's opinions or feelings.

Authoritative parents tend to be focused on controlling their children and thrive on verbalizing their authority over others.

Authoritarian parents are cold and unaccepting. They often utilize threats and shaming. They punish rather than discipline and would rather have kids be sorry for their mistakes rather than learn a better way to behave in the future. They justify their actions by telling others that they are helping their child to "toughen up." They are convinced that their actions are helping their child to adopt a "desired" belief system. This typically means that they are teaching their child to blindly accept the beliefs that the authoritarian parent has deemed acceptable, without questioning or challenging those beliefs. Children of authoritarian parents have been demonstrated to have increased aggression and decreased self-esteem.

Authoritarian cliff notes: low responsiveness and high demandingness. Tends to lead to kids who have behavioral problems. They may have more temper tantrums, are less independent, and have low self-esteem. They may struggle in social situations and are at higher risk for substance abuse.

In my experience, these are kids who either grow up to mimic their parents' behavior without question or who completely resent their parents. The latter cut off communication. They choose not to have a relationship with a person who cared more about being the boss and engaging in power trips rather than successfully raising a child to become a confident, well-adjusted adult.

My son's former friend has an authoritarian parent. She was the boss of her home and was very proud of that distinction. She demanded absolute compliance with her rules and didn't want to hear about it if her child questioned those rules. It was her way or the highway. She was always right, even when she wasn't. Let's be real. She was an absolute bitch who thrived on power trips.

Her oldest son had a tendency to lie. He convinced other people that he and my son were actually cousins. One day when I picked my son up from his school's aftercare program, a mom approached me and said, "Oh, you're Mason's mom and Justin's aunt!" By the way,

Justin is not his real name. I had to inform her that while I was in fact Mason's mom, his "cousin" was not related to us.

As he grew older, authoritarian mom's son developed more and more behavioral problems. He would bully other kids. At times he would act out physically. If his behavior was within his mom's expectations, he would be praised, even if his behavior hurt another child. If his behavior was unacceptable according to mom, he would be punished.

Their friendship came to a breaking point when Mason slugged "Mr. liar, liar, pants on fire." The incident was witnessed by multiple adults. The consensus was that the child had been verbally attacking Mason for days, at recess and at the after-school program. Mason hit his breaking point and lashed out. Physical aggression is not something that my husband and I ever condone. We teach our kids to keep their hands to themselves. However, in this particular situation, everyone was in agreement that Mason only acted out because he was provoked.

Authoritarian mom was not happy that her son was felt to be at fault. Instead of acting like an adult and calling me to discuss the situation, she posted an insanely long tantrum on social media about how she did not care how intelligent her children were; she just wanted them to "act like Jesus" and was convinced that their actions were in line with this principle. She described the incident in incredible detail, to the point that others could tell my son was involved even though she never mentioned him by name.

Don't be like an authoritarian mom. Her kids are screwed.

Permissive Parenting

A third parenting style is called permissive. A permissive parent demonstrates high responsiveness and low demandingness. Permissive parents are great at responding to their child's needs. They are warm and accepting. The inherent problem with a permissive parent is that they allow their child to be in charge. Permissive parents relinquish their authority to their child; the child becomes the boss of the family. This is not a good thing.

Permissive parents often provide little guidance related to acceptable behavior. They may set rules, but they don't enforce them. They infrequently provide consequences for negative behavior and rarely follow through on implementing said consequences. Permissive parents are overly lenient. If their child behaves in an inappropriate manner, the parent will make excuses for them. Problematic behavior demonstrated by their child is never their child's fault; someone else is always in the wrong.

Permissive parents overindulge, overpraise, and overprotect their child. They jump through hoops to ensure their child's comfort and happiness. If you have ever come across a parent who repeatedly says, "It's (*insert child's name here*) world, we're all just living in it," they are likely a permissive parent.

I have had numerous permissive parents in my medical practice over the years, but one particular family takes the cake. One time, they brought their child in to see me for ear pain. In order for me to appropriately diagnose an ear infection, I have to look into a child's ear and view their tympanic membrane. Using an otoscope to look into an ear causes no discomfort. It can be a little scary for some kids, but usually, a brief explanation about it being pain-free leads to compliance with this medical tool. Not for this family. These parents acted like I had asked their child to donate a kidney when I simply asked to look into his ears.

Instead of trying to be helpful, these parents tried to appease their child, which led to the child kicking and screaming while covering his ears. It took two medical assistants to safely hold him down in order for me to provide an appropriate physical examination. After I was finished, instead of disciplining their child for inappropriate behavior, they offered to buy him McDonald's for being a "good boy" because he allowed the doctor to look into his ears.

In my experience, children of permissive parents are prone to develop into adults who are entitled, selfish, and demanding. They expect others to take responsibility for their inappropriate actions. They tend to struggle with rules and expectations, because such expectations should not have to apply to them. At the same time, they tend to look for a reward simply for engaging in appropriate behavior. They perceive themselves to be more "special" than others, because that is what their parents taught them. These are teenagers who start a part-time job, only to quit because their boss refused to let them take a break every hour.

Children of permissive parents have been shown to have a higher degree of impulsivity as well as a higher risk for developing cavities and obesity. They struggle with self-control and tend to continue egocentric behaviors far past the stage of egocentrism being developmentally appropriate.

Permissive cliff notes: high responsiveness and low demandingness. These kids may have lower overall academic achievement and may struggle with relationships with their peers.

Neglectful Parenting

The final parenting style is called uninvolved or neglectful. These parents possess low responsiveness and low demandingness. A neglectful parent does not spend much time with their kids. They are cold and indifferent. They don't nurture their children and often have little knowledge as to what their children are doing. They are not responsive to their child's physical, emotional, or social needs. They do not set expectations for behavior and provide little to no supervision.

These are parents who may not want to take on parental duties. They skip important events like parent-teacher conferences. If they are willing to sign their kids up for participation in sports, they do not attend games. They may utilize teasing or shaming if a child attempts to get physical or emotional needs met.

It's important to note that some neglectful parents may not parent in this way intentionally. They may have been raised by a neglectful parent and are just doing what they know. Other times, neglectful parents are caught up in their own issues—alcohol or drug abuse, severe mental illness, or working multiple jobs to keep a roof over their family's head. In many cases, the circumstances that lead to neglectful parenting are not something that anyone actually desires, so please reserve judgment.

Children of neglectful parents have been found to have decreased self-esteem, decreased school performance, and increased risk of drug abuse. They are at higher risk for depression and anxiety. They often struggle to form secure attachments. They are more likely to commit minor crimes during adolescence. They often have to learn how to take care of themselves, and possibly their siblings.

Here's an example of a neglectful parent brought to my attention by a school nurse. The nurse wanted to clarify the child's ADHD medication administration. I had written a note instructing the school nurse to administer the medication immediately upon arrival at school and again at noon. Normally, I recommend that parents administer ADHD medication at home, but this mom insisted on administration at school.

Once I spoke to the nurse, I realized that mom did not drop the child off at school until around 10:30 a.m., if she brought him to school at all. The school day started at 8:00 a.m. The nurse was concerned about administering the medication at 10:30 a.m. and again at noon, and rightfully so. Had this nurse failed to contact me, this child may have had significant problems related to his medication.

Oftentimes, I am not a witness to a neglectful parent's behavior. After all, the act of bringing a child to a doctor's appointment, especially for a well-child exam, indicates that the parent is not neglectful. Appearances may be deceiving. Neglectful parents may fly under the radar unless a concerned party is involved. If a child seems to be neglected by their parents, the other loved ones in their life need to speak up.

The most gut-wrenching example of the outcomes of neglectful parenting comes from a set of siblings in my medical practice. They had been placed into foster care because their parent was running a drug house. During their first visit with me, the older sister jumped up onto the sink in the exam room, stuck her head under the faucet, and turned it on. She didn't realize that she could ask for a cup of water.

As these children grew up, the sister was unable to form secure attachments. She had a fear of being abandoned. She constantly pushed people away with her words and her actions; she left them before they could leave her. She acted cold and aloof. The only person she seemed to care about was her younger brother.

Her brother had a better outcome, thanks to her. While his sister had to fend for herself, she also took care of her brother and provided for his needs as best she could. As a result, he did have the ability to form semi-secure attachments. Overall, he had a much more positive view of the world. He was more trusting and less aloof. He had his own struggles, but they were nowhere near as severe as his sister's struggles.

Uninvolved cliff notes: low responsiveness and low demandingness. These are kids who are left to fend for themselves. The severity of neglect may necessitate a referral to child protective services.

Authoritarian, permissive, and neglectful styles are potentially damaging. They will prevent a child from reaching their true potential. And unfortunately, most parents who fall into these categories have no idea that they are being detrimental to their child's development. However, if you realize that you are anything other than an authoritative parent, congratulations on your self-awareness. I implore you to seek help. Find a therapist. Get your own stressful life under control. I know that this is much easier said than done. Your child deserves better, and so do you.

Is the Baumrind/Maccoby and Martin theory outdated? For sure! Baumrind's research was performed on white middle-class Americans in the 1960s. A lack of diversity and a lack of exploring different cultural perspectives are limitations to this theory. However, all theories have limitations. The idea is to choose the information that resonates with you and your family and utilize it to create more effective ways to parent your child.

Although this theory may be outdated, it is still very useful. It breaks down different styles of parenting very simply and provides a nice foundation for understanding discipline. Is this theory conceptually perfect? Of course not! I'm sure that there are developmental and behavioral psychologists who will rip Baumrind's theory to shreds. But as a pediatrician and a mom, I find it to be useful and applicable.

Let me give you one final example of how this parenting style theory plays out in real life. Let's meet a little boy named Johnny. Johnny is typically sweet and kind, though he is a strong-willed five-year-old. And while he normally loves going to school, one day he decides he wants to stay home even though both of his parents have to go to work. He throws a fit, crosses his arm, stomps his feet, and yells, "I AM NOT GOING TO SCHOOL!!!" His parents respond in the following ways:

- *Authoritative Parent*: You seem really mad today. And I am sorry that you do not want to go to school. But Mommy and Daddy both have to go to work even though we don't want to. And you have to go to school. Would you like to help me pack your lunch?
- *Authoritarian Parent*: You are going to school today and that is final! Now get your coat, put on your shoes and get into the car right now! If you don't, I will take away your Legos for the next month!
- *Permissive Parent*: Oh Sweetie, Mommy is supposed to go to work today. I guess I'll call my boss and pretend to be sick so we can stay home together. If you don't want to go to school, you don't have to. It's only kindergarten. And yes, we can go to Burger King for lunch.
- *Neglectful/Uninvolved Parent*: Whatever. I don't care. Do what you want. Just don't interrupt me when I'm watching TV. And don't expect me to make you lunch—you know where the food is.

Most of the time, I consider myself an authoritative parent. However, if one of my kids runs into the street without looking for traffic, I turn into an authoritarian really fast. And then I switch back into authoritative mode and explain why I screamed my head off. But instead of focusing on which of the four parenting styles you embody, I suggest that you focus on the traits that define these styles.

Are you loving and warm? Do you have clear, consistent expectations for your child? Do you follow through on enforcing consequences for breaking the rules? Are your actions as a parent intended to teach and guide or to punish and shame? You cannot possibly prepare for every challenge that you will face as a parent. But if you are able to focus on responsiveness and demandingness, parenting becomes a little easier.

I strongly encourage you to develop high responsiveness and high demandingness. And not because it pushes you into the authoritarian category. The name of the style isn't important, and labels don't mean much to successful parents. I want you to strive for this because it helps you to demonstrate the attributes that will help your child or children thrive as they progress through life.

23

The Challenges
Co-Parenting and Parenting Siblings

Co-Parenting

It takes two people to create a child. Some children are the products of one-night stands, and others are born out of long-term, committed relationships. But life is complicated. It's not uncommon for the two people who bring a child into this world or who adopt a child to decide to part ways to no longer be in a romantic relationship with each other. That is life.

This wasn't always the case; in the past, countless people stayed together because of religious or social pressure. When I was growing up, my maternal grandparents hated each other. In fact, "hate" may not be a strong enough word to describe their feelings toward each other.

Growing up, I never heard my maternal grandmother call my maternal grandfather by his name; instead, she would refer to him as "that bastard." Apparently, this hatred started decades before I was born. I've been told that my maternal grandmother never wanted children. She ended up having six. Back in the 1940s when my grandparents first married, divorce was unheard of, at least in their community. So, they stayed married, even though they could not stand to be in the same room together. Holidays were always interesting, but that's another story for another time.

By the time I was born, my grandparents were not living together. My grandmother lived in the family home, and my grandfather lived in an apartment that he owned above his dental practice. They had nothing nice to say about each other, avoided each other at all costs, and family get-togethers were very uncomfortable. I'd like to believe that my grandparents were at least decent to each other when my mom and her siblings were growing up, but I doubt it.

When two parents are no longer in a romantic relationship with each other, yet share the care of a child, co-parenting comes into play. It's beyond the scope of this book to explain all the nuances that are involved; it can be incredibly complex. I empathize, and, to a certain degree, I understand the challenges involved. Yet I do know one single fact. Successful co-parenting involves putting the child first. It involves being willing to cooperate and compromise with a person you may not like. It means putting your own feelings aside in order to raise another human being to the best of your abilities.

I have seen parent-parent and parent-child interactions of thousands and thousands of co-parenting families over the course of my career. Some are amazing at putting their differences aside for the sake of their child. Others are complete disasters and are hell-bent on hurting the other parent at all costs. Let me give you a few examples.

The first example is a family who is determined to put their child first. This family includes one child, a biological mom, a stepmom, and a biological father. The family had 50/50 shared custody. The biological mom and stepmom texted each other frequently when it came to the care of the child. They attended doctor's appointments and parent-teacher conferences together. They refrained from saying mean, hurtful things about the other parent in front of the child.

These women are not friends. In fact, they really do not like each other. Yet, they work hard not to show their dislike, especially in front of the child. The adults involved are completely committed to raising the child in the best way possible.

Another example is a family where the two parents are stuck in the hurt and pain that came from experiences in their romantic relationship. They can't or won't get past the pain, and they are more concerned with being the "better" parent rather than focusing on the needs of the child or children involved. These types of families struggle to co-parent effectively, and as a result, their child or children suffer. The adults involved point fingers at the other parent instead of focusing on their child. They blame, they complain, and they may use excessive sarcasm. They deflect rather than become introspective. They say things to insinuate how much "better" they are at parenting.

Passive aggressiveness is a key feature of parents who are struggling to co-parent. Any time I witness passive-aggressive behavior from parents, I know that the child is not being put first. Statements such as "In my house we . . ." or "At her mom's house, they don't . . ." are the biggest offenders. I want you to understand that passive aggressiveness does not make you a better parent. It does not give you a one-up. It only hurts the child or children involved. Remember, children crave consistency. When you make it a point to pit one home against the other home, that is the opposite of consistency.

In my medical practice, there are many times when I have felt uncomfortable because of the degree of tension I feel from co-parenting parents. At times, it gets hostile. On more than one occasion, a family has tried to get me involved in their drama, and I always refuse to engage in parental disagreements. I cannot say this to families in my medical practice, even though at times I really want to. The most important advice that I can give to those involved in co-parenting situations is not for the faint of heart. Are you ready?

With all due respect, get over yourself. The truth is that it is not about you. It's about your beautiful child (or children). You may be hurting. You may feel betrayed. You may cry on a daily basis. I am so sorry for your pain, but the difficult reality is that co-parenting is not about you. It's about your child.

I don't mean to be harsh. I am not trying to diminish your personal hardships. I have no idea what you have gone through, and there is certainly no judgment here. But I have had so many patients over the years who became a shell of the person they once were because they were trying to please parents with completely different expectations, rules, and belief systems. These children end up walking on eggshells. They become so hyper-focused on what each parent wants from them, and about what is expected in each household, that they lose themselves. They try so hard to anticipate, and to meet, divergent expectations. This is exhausting for a child.

If you are in a co-parenting situation, you need to put your hurt, your grievances, and your pain aside. I am so sorry if your previous partner cheated on you, stole money from you, or treated you in an abusive manner. If that is the case, make sure to seek healing. Find a counselor, get acupuncture, or start taking a kickboxing class. It's incredibly important that you take care of yourself. It's very important that you seek out experiences that can help you heal.

But at the same time, please realize that none of those situations has anything to do with your child. Take the time to heal, but make sure to stay focused on the child or children involved. What is best for the kids and what is the evidence to support it?

Successful co-parenting means that you and the other person who created your child are committed to putting aside your differences in order to parent the child you created. You don't ignore your past experiences, but you also don't involve your child in those experiences. You can't change the past, but you can have significant control over the future.

It's important to have a predetermined schedule. The consistency benefits your child, and being able to count on the other parent to keep commitments leads to improved communication. At the same time, it's important to be flexible and understanding when unforeseen situations arise. Communication with the other parent and with the child involved is crucial when schedules change.

Successful co-parents avoid being manipulative. It's important that people in co-parenting situations are not threatened by love or affection that the child shows to other parents, and they don't try to influence their child into making them the "favorite" parent. They don't bad-mouth the other parent or say disparaging things. They maintain a "if you don't have anything nice to say, don't say anything at all" approach.

In addition, successful co-parents attempt to find a basic agreement about important issues—their child's health, schooling, discipline strategies, and spiritual upbringing. They avoid fighting in front of their child. Ideally, people who are co-parenting have thought about, and created a plan, to handle disagreements related to the health and well-being of the child.

All of these things may be a lot easier said than done. Maybe your child's father is a complete narcissist who cares about no one other than himself. Maybe your child's mother is hell-bent on making you the bad guy because she blames you for the divorce. Maybe your child's dad wants to be a friend to your child instead of acting like a parent.

Maybe you found out that your ex-wife was cheating because you took your kid for a haircut. He looked at the kid in the chair next to him and said, "Oh hey brother. Dad, my brother is here." It took a few minutes, but you finally realized that "brother" is the child of the man your wife was having an affair with. Sounds unreal? It happened to a family I know.

You cannot control anyone but yourself. At the same time, you cannot throw in the towel. Your child is depending on you. There are productive ways to initiate conversations about co-parenting issues. You just need to be proactive about it.

I strongly suggest that co-parents sit down (with lawyers if needed) to discuss communication between both parties. Communication is essential when it comes to co-parenting a child. Have a conversation with your child's other parent as to the preferred form of communication. Will you speak over the phone? Send text messages? Send emails? Use an app on your cell phone? Decide this together.

I also strongly suggest that you choose in-person or over-the-phone conversations, especially if you are upset with the other person. Face-to-face communication is more effective than communication via text or email. Yet I have several families in my medical practice that are legally bound to communicate solely through a parenting app. If you choose, or are mandated, to communicate via text, email, or through an app, try to stay calm and be straightforward. In addition, be clear, concise, and respectful. If you are texting, do not use all capital letters, as it gives the appearance that you are shouting.

For co-parents who have a contentious relationship, you may want to create communication rules. Here are some examples of helpful communication rules:

- Commit to speaking in a calm and rational manner.
- If a parent starts to feel angry or overwhelmed, they should walk away and disengage until they are calm.
- Communication should avoid aggression, name-calling, blame, and swearing.
- All communication needs to be focused on the child.

Effective communication will make co-parenting much easier. A simple transition to make is to pay attention to the words "I" and "You." I want to take a moment to discuss "I" statements. An "I" statement is very much what it sounds like; it is a statement that starts with the word "I."

The easiest way to explain how "I" statements are beneficial is to explain how "You" statements are detrimental. Anytime you start a statement with the word "You," you are immediately putting the other person on edge. The very mention of the word "You" has caused the other person's brain to go into fight-flight-freeze mode.

Here's an example. Imagine that your child arrives late to school on the days that the other parent is responsible for school drop-off. If you tell the other parent, "You are constantly bringing them to school late!" I bet that will not be perceived well. An argument may ensue. You may want to consider saying, "I am concerned that (*child's name*) has been late to school. Can you help me understand what is going on? I'm happy to help." This communication is much more child-centered and less aggressive.

A non-aggressive communication style may take time to develop and that is okay! It is going to take trial and error. Sometimes the way in which we phrase statements has a profound impact. Let me give you some examples of lead statements that may improve communication:

- I think we should do what's best for (*child's name here*). I'm interested in your thoughts on . . .
- I want to work with you. Can we please try to put our differences aside for (*child's name here*)?
- (*Child's name here*) is interested in taking a dance class. Do you think we could work that into our schedules?
- (*Child's name here*) has a parent-teacher conference on November 21. I'd really like for us to attend together. Do you think you can make it?

Co-parenting can be incredibly challenging. Every interaction that you have with your child's other parent is an opportunity to improve your communication skills. Again, as long as the primary focus is on the child or children involved, you are on the right track.

Parenting Siblings

As if raising one child wasn't hard enough, many of us parents bring multiple children into this world. Talk about exponential challenges! Please understand and accept that each of your children needs you to parent them in slightly different ways. Remember, it's important to have a child-centered focus, which means that you may treat your children differently. You may have different expectations for each of your children. You may love them in different ways. If that's the case, good for you! The most successful behavioral expectations are determined based on age, developmental skills, social and emotional development, and temperament.

Once my son turned eleven years old, my husband and I expected him to take daily showers and use deodorant on a regular basis. Meanwhile, his eight-year-old sister took a bath every other day. My son determined that this was unfair. We had a meeting with him to explain the reasons for the differences in expectations regarding personal hygiene, and he responded well to that explanation.

It's important to have discussions with your child about why you have different expectations for them and for their siblings. This does not mean that you change your expectations because your child is not on board. Rather, it means that you involve your children in appropriate conversations about behavior and take the time to understand and address your child's unique point of view. You are the adult, and you get to make the decisions. However, those decisions will either help or hurt your child. Make sure to try to understand and accommodate their perspective when you create expectations.

It is almost a guarantee that one child is easier to parent than your other child or children. Maybe they actually listen to you and do what you ask the first time. Maybe they are more willing to go to bed, or to eat your cooking, or to clean their room. Maybe they are less emotionally reactive, more go-with-the-flow, or have a temperament that aligns with a goodness of fit to your temperament. These are the children that often provide us with a proverbial fresh breath of air.

Here is a parenting truth that may be difficult to accept. The "easier" child will automatically be perceived as the favorite child by their siblings. Kids are smart. If you parent the easier child with less discipline because they require less discipline, this will be perceived as favoritism. If the easier child has a better temperamental goodness of fit with their parents, this will also be perceived as favoritism.

Siblings will assume that the favorite child is more loved than they are and inherently better than they are. I understand that as a parent, this may be difficult to comprehend. I have no doubt that you love all of your children deeply. Yet, you express that love in different ways. That is normal and does not need to change.

However, you may need to go out of your way to explain these differences to your children. Remember, kids do not have a fully developed brain. Their perceptions are based on their experiences, and your child's perception is their reality. This may or may not be consistent with your reality. Please make an extra effort to communicate with the more difficult child or children that they are not less loved, or less than in any way, compared to the easier child.

Here is an example. My brother and I are five and a half years apart in age. I'm the oldest child. Growing up, my mom put my socks on my brother's feet every day until he was about eleven years old. She always seemed to be smiling at him as she performed this mundane task. My underdeveloped brain perceived this daily interaction as an expression of her loving my brother more than me.

Was that an accurate assessment of the situation? I'll never know. However, because I was not encouraged to have open, honest conversations with my parents, I spent far too many years believing that my mom loved my brother more than me, because I had to put my own socks on and he didn't. It seems silly, but I can guarantee you that your kids will perceive some discrepancy in your behavior as favoritism.

The challenge in raising multiple children is that while you are attempting to parent each child individually, your children are watching you and comparing your parenting behaviors. They may complain about minor discrepancies. Your best defense is to be on the offense. Explain why you have different expectations for each child. Explain your approach to individual discipline in developmentally appropriate terms. Involve them in discussions about expected behaviors.

Every once in a while, check in with each child individually. Do they feel that they are being treated fairly? Do they feel loved and that they are an important member of the family? Do they have any questions about different expectations?

Despite your best efforts, your children still may challenge the differences. That's okay. To this day, my children often remind me, "Mom! I can put my own socks on!" No parent is perfect. Stay focused on your child's unique cognitive, emotional, and social development, as well as their temperament. Be willing to discuss why you parent one child differently than another child. Finally, keep growing and learning.

PART VIII

MAKING IT HAPPEN

24

Discipline Based on Age

It's time to put it all together. We are going to use the concepts of development and temperament in order to create the best parenting strategy for your unique child or children. I am going to use an age-based approach, but please understand that the concepts exist on a continuum and are not limited to a specific age. For example, what works best for your two-year-old may work best for someone else's three-year-old.

Birth to Twelve Months Old

From birth to age three, over one million neural connections are formed every second. This period is crucial to set the stage for successful development. Experiences are everything at this age. Make sure to respond to your child's needs, both physically and emotionally. Engage with your child by interacting with them. Talk to them, sing to them, and read to them. Allow them the opportunity to explore the world around them, and provide a safe, nurturing, and loving environment.

There is no such thing as spoiling an infant. Crying is one of the only ways that infants are able to demonstrate that they need something. They are not trying to be manipulative by crying; they are asking for help. It's very important to respond to those cries. Getting their needs met helps an infant to feel secure and helps them to understand that the world around them is safe. They don't even realize the cause-and-effect relationship between crying and getting something they need until around nine months of age.

Infants usually do not need discipline, because they don't have many behavior problems. They usually can't walk, and they are just learning to talk. They are cute, they are cuddly, and even though they are a lot of work, they are also really fun. I say this as a fellow parent and with all of the love in my heart, but problematic behavior during infancy is usually caused by parents, not baby. This is because some parents have unrealistic expectations during the first year of their child's life.

Sleep deprivation is very real for parents of infants. Many parents want their baby to sleep through the night, even though young infants need to eat every two to four hours to grow properly. Expecting an infant to sleep through the night is unrealistic. If it does happen, it's probably due to a combination of temperament and luck. You can encourage good sleep habits, but you can't force a baby to sleep. You may need to reframe your expectations about infant sleep. And remember, do not compare your infant to other infants.

Other parents are tired of the never-ending laundry and have trouble accepting that their baby's spitting up is actually normal. The truth is that the great majority of infants spit up, and many may spit up multiple times per day. It's a mess, it's inconvenient, but again, it's unrealistic to expect an infant to never spit up. When my daughter was four months old, she usually needed four outfits per day, because she spit up all the time. It was annoying, but eventually resolved on its own.

When it comes to the successful parenting of infants, try to learn your baby's cues. Do your best to meet their physical, emotional, and social needs. Ask for help when needed. Above all, make sure that your expectations are in line with your child's abilities. If you aren't sure of what to expect, ask your pediatrician!

Twelve Months to Four Years Old

These are challenging years for parents! True problematic behavior tends to start during the toddler and preschool years. Children at this age want to be independent, yet lack the physical, emotional, and social skills to actually act independently. This is when temper tantrums start, when biting may happen, and when children first start challenging the authority of their parents.

Remember, the ability to have rational thought is almost nonexistent at this age. Toddlers and preschoolers are egocentric and lack the ability to look at the world from another person's perspective. They want attention, even if that attention is not positive. Ignoring minor infractions, such as throwing food on the floor, will help the unwanted behavior extinguish faster than trying to address it.

In addition, toddlers lack coping skills to deal with being tired, hungry, stressed, or overwhelmed. Coping skills involve using conscious effort to minimize or tolerate stress and discomfort. Such skills require a developed neocortex, which toddlers and preschoolers do not have. Your best bet is to try to avoid triggers for misbehavior.

Ignoring and redirecting are some of the most effective responses to certain forms of unwanted behavior. If you notice that little Joey is about to color a wall with crayon, I suggest you stay calm, ignore the crayon and exclaim, "Oh my goodness, look at this new book Joey! Let's read it together." Help the child focus their attention on something other than the naughty thing they were about to do. This is called redirection.

That was a lot of information. Let's summarize. Toddlers and preschoolers crave attention, and ignoring their behaviors eliminates any type of attention. Ignoring minor behavioral infractions can be immensely helpful at extinguishing unwanted behaviors, such as throwing food on the floor, to resolve.

In addition to ignoring, redirecting your child's attention may help eliminate unwanted behaviors. Redirection involves providing a new focus for your child's attention. Instead of shrieking at your child for attempting to draw on a wall, ask them to color a picture for you instead. It's important to understand that while some unwanted behaviors can be prevented with ignoring and redirection, problematic behavior is still going to occur.

Aggressive behaviors, such as hitting, kicking, biting, and throwing things, should never be ignored. The first step to addressing aggressive behavior is to understand that it is an expression of the fight-flight-freeze response. Young children need their space and do not appreciate spatial relations in the same way that adults do. They will act out if they feel like someone has invaded their turf. Please view aggressive behavior as an expression of an overwhelmed brain. This helps to set appropriate behavioral expectations.

Successfully managing aggressive behavior requires a specific skill set, yet there is wiggle room in the process I am going to suggest. Take a few deep breaths before you respond to the aggression. Staying calm is essential. Put on a poker face. Remember, kids want attention. If you have a big reaction to their behavior, you are only encouraging that behavior to continue.

Get into position. Crouch down, look your child in the eyes, and say something like "No hitting! Hitting hurts!" Then walk away from the hitter, yet remain within their line of sight until they have calmed down. Shift your focus to the person who was hit. Hug them, kiss them, and tell them how sorry you are that they got hurt. Just don't mention the name of the hitter when you are doing this.

Once the situation has been defused, reflect on the reason that your child engaged in hitting behavior. Did they want a cup of milk instead of a cup of water? Did someone steal their toy? Are they hungry or tired?

When everyone is calm and happy, make sure to label your child's emotions. Explain why the behavior was wrong and suggest a replacement skill. For example, "It looks like you were really mad when Mommy gave you a cup of milk. It is okay to be mad, but it is not okay to hit. Hitting hurts. If you would like water, please say water." Obviously, this is a very specific approach that I encourage you to modify based on your unique child's temperament. This is meant to be a guide.

Let's discuss the concept of time-outs as a discipline tool. When implemented intentionally, time-outs can be effective at diminishing or extinguishing an unwanted behavior. A time-out involves removing a child from an environment that reinforces an unwanted behavior and moving them to an environment that does not reinforce the unwanted behavior. Lack of stimulation, lack of parental attention, and time to self-regulate are features of effective time-outs. Effective time-outs are intended to be brief and boring.

If you want to use time-outs in an effective manner, you need to be calm, consistent, and persistent. You need to explain the concept of a time-out to your child when they are calm and in a good mood. You need to discuss the specific behaviors that will result in a time-out. My suggestion is to limit time-outs to two to four specific problematic behaviors at the most.

When your child engages in a time-out-worthy behavior, you provide one, and only one, warning to them. If they stop the behavior, you praise them. If they don't, you immediately put them into a time-out. You do not talk to your child during a time-out. If they cry during a time-out, you do not respond. Once your child calms down, that signals the end of the time-out. Time-outs are endorsed by the American Academy of Pediatrics and are an effective discipline strategy.

However, time-outs quickly turn into punishment if implemented incorrectly. If a parent yells or engages in other hostile behavior during a time-out, children often perceive time-outs as a rejection. Coupled with the social isolation inherent to time-outs, they may cause a child to feel shame. When someone experiences shame, they believe that they are bad or wrong, instead of their behavior being bad or wrong.

Lack of consistency and unrealistic expectations will turn time-outs into a disaster quickly. Threatening to give a time-out multiple times, not implementing the time-out immediately after the misbehavior occurs, and giving up on time-outs because they did not "work" after a few attempts are all examples of lack of consistency. In addition, expecting a child to "think about" their misbehavior during a time-out and expecting a child to stay in the time-out space without leaving are also examples of unrealistic time-out expectations.

Recently, the concept of a "time-in" has come into play. A time-in involves sitting with your child and inviting them to express their feelings while providing them an opportunity to calm themselves down. The key difference is that the parent stays with the child during a time-in, whereas a time-out involves parent-child separation.

I'll be honest. I hate time-outs, and I hate time-ins. Why? They promise improved behavior with techniques that are likely implemented incorrectly. Furthermore, they do not provide any instruction as to how a child could behave more appropriately in the future. Remember, the human brain needs to know what to do. Telling it what not to do is not helpful. Any discipline during this age absolutely needs to include a brief explanation of how a parent would like the child to behave in the future.

Finally, monitor and modify your child's environment. Kids are sponges, and they absorb everything. Are they watching a YouTube video that involves hitting? Are you watching the evening news while they are still awake? Look for every single possible exposure to violence or aggression or emotional meltdowns and then get rid of it.

At the same time, please praise your child's positive behaviors! Acknowledging and praising behaviors that you want to continue will, in fact, encourage those behaviors to continue. This seems obvious, yet it may be challenging to put into practice. You may need to praise your child for behaviors that you already expect to be demonstrated consistently, such as saying, "Please" or "Thank You." Praise, praise, and praise more if your toddler or preschooler engages in a behavior that you want them to continue.

Five to Eleven Years Old

If I had to choose a single word to describe the most effective discipline strategy for this age range, it would be collaboration. Developing a collaborative relationship with your child does not mean that you are not in charge. It does not mean that you give in to your child's demands. Rather, it means that you attempt to view the world from your child's perspective, give them a voice to explain any unwanted behaviors that they demonstrate, and provide consequences for misbehavior that are congruent with their age, developmental skills, and severity of the behavior. You explain the problematic behavior, suggest ways to improve their behavior in the future, and explain the reasons for providing and implementing the consequences for the unwanted behavior.

Let's go through an example. You get a phone call from your child's school that your ten-year-old child got into a scuffle with another child at recess. Your child pushed the other child, who fell down and banged his head. Initially, you are livid. You are embarrassed. You cannot believe that your child put his hands on another child, after all the discussions that you have had about conflict resolution.

Yet you are committed to a child-centered approach. You take a few deep breaths on your way to the school. You use your duck-on-a-pond imagery. You remind yourself to remain neutral and to listen to the information presented about the incident from all parties, without judgment. You recognize that your child will probably shut down in front of the principal and say, "I don't know," when asked why he pushed another child. You remain calm, choose your words carefully, and then set up a family meeting (without siblings) for later that day.

During the family meeting, your child explains his perspective again, which is congruent with his explanation in the principal's office. He explains that there was mutual trash-talk while playing soccer at recess. Eventually, the other child involved tried to punch him, so he pushed the child to defend himself. You thank your child for telling his truth and determine an appropriate consequence for his part in the incident. What exactly is the best, most instructional consequence for pushing another child at recess?

I wish it was that simple. The exact specifics of the consequence implemented will depend on your family mission statement, your beliefs about self-defense and conflict resolution, and your child's unique temperament. Providing appropriate discipline that encourages improved behavior in the future can be complicated! No one does this perfectly. Do your best, be open-minded, and learn from each experience.

If this were my child, I would praise him for his honesty. Honesty is valued in our home, and his consistent explanations suggest he is, in fact, being truthful. In addition, he would be praised for defending himself. If another child was trying to punch my child, I wouldn't want them to do nothing. At the same time, he would be admonished for putting his hands onto another child, which is not the way we resolve conflict in our home. Finally, my husband and I would ask our child how he could respond to the same situation in a more positive manner in the future.

The consequence for the misbehavior would depend on our child's response to the above question. If the response was "I would push him to the ground again!" we would likely take away his PlayStation for a week, have him watch some videos about successful conflict resolution, and discuss better behavioral responses in the future. On the other hand, if the answer was "I would say, 'Not cool bro!' and then I would walk away," we may simply praise this, remind him not to put his hands on another child, and encourage him to seek a recess attendant in the future.

Twelve to Eighteen Years Old

Being the parent of a teenager is not for the faint of heart. One of the challenges during this phase is that your child's appearance may be that of a full-grown adult. They may have facial hair, be taller than you, or may be successfully juggling school, sports, and an after-school job. Yet their brain still has a lot of developing to do. To make matters more challenging, there are certain behaviors that may negatively affect a teenager's developing brain. Understanding this can help you teach your child that they are not ready to engage in certain grown-up behaviors.

At the same time, I want you to expect your teenager to assume that you are an idiot and that they know more than you. Don't take this behavior personally. In fact, this is the time to dig in and fight for consistency. You may be tempted to act more like a friend to your child given how mature they may seem at times. Don't do it. Your teenager needs parents who provide the same level of security and consistency that they provided a decade ago. You cannot allow your child to take a few sips of alcohol at a family function and then punish them for drinking with their friends after prom. Successful parenting doesn't work like that.

The same child-centered approach discussed with the five to eleven-year-olds still applies to teenagers. However, this is the stage where teenage behaviors may be unsafe. Such behaviors need to be addressed in developmentally appropriate ways.

Let's go through an example. You find out that your sixteen-year-old has been smoking marijuana with her friends. You are horrified. You are scared. Your gut instinct is to lock her in her room and never let her spend time with those "friends" ever again. Yet you know that this approach will backfire. You take a few deep breaths and make a game plan.

Before you address your child's behavior, you need to make sure that you understand marijuana inside and out. Kids are smart and will see through attempts at being inauthentic. If you try to discipline them about something you know little about, you will lose all credibility. Therefore, you need to understand the chemical components, the effects, and the potential dangers of marijuana use.

Without this knowledge, it will be challenging to help your child understand why they need to stop using marijuana. Do your homework; do a Google search of reputable sources if you need to. Once you have a solid understanding of how marijuana affects the body, request a meeting with your child.

During the meeting, do your best to stay calm. The first objective of this meeting is for you to gather information. You ask open-ended questions about your child's marijuana use. You try to understand their actions from their perspective. What caused them to start smoking marijuana in the first place? Without putting words into their mouth, try to determine if peer pressure, curiosity, or a desire to relieve anxiety played a role.

If they have smoked marijuana on multiple occasions, what caused them to repeat the behavior? What does your child understand about the short- and long-term effects of marijuana use? You listen to your child's answers without judgment. You acknowledge and validate any emotions that your child demonstrates. In fact, I encourage you to take notes. This demonstrates that you are actively listening to your child.

At the same time, you are concerned about your child's safety, and you express this to them. After the information-gathering phase, you gently explain your specific concerns. You discuss that regular marijuana use will lead to problems with memory, coordination, reaction time, and difficulty with problem-solving. You remind your child that marijuana is sometimes laced with more serious, and often deadly, substances such as fentanyl. You gently remind them that because their brain is not fully developed, regular marijuana use will cause brain damage. You don't mention anything about your past experiences with substance use, whether it be marijuana, alcohol, or something else, because it's not about you.

Now it's time for the most challenging aspect of parenting—providing an appropriate consequence for a misbehavior that helps your child understand how to act more appropriately in the future. I wish I could tell you the best consequence to provide a child who is smoking marijuana or engaging in any type of unsafe, detrimental behavior. I can't. For this example, the consequence for smoking marijuana depends on so many individual factors, including your child's temperament, intent, pattern of use, and family belief system. Effective discipline of this particular issue also involves determining how to discourage your child's use of marijuana in the future. It may take trial and error. That's okay.

If this situation occurred in my home, a family meeting would be scheduled, though the only participants would be myself, my husband, and the child who decided to use marijuana. The goal of the family meeting is to understand my child's reason for using marijuana. One of the consequences I would implement would involve my child sitting down with me and watching educational videos about the history of marijuana and its negative effects when used by teenagers. We would then have a future family meeting to discuss the risks and benefits of marijuana use. Because the risks of marijuana use in teenagers far outweigh the benefits, further consequences for future marijuana use would be discussed and enforced. My children value participation in sports, so the effects of marijuana on sports performance would be included in these discussions. Once we identified the reasons for the marijuana use, we would discuss how to behave more positively and healthily in the future. And then my husband and I would watch our child like a hawk to monitor for future marijuana use. If it occurred, the entire process would be repeated. Is this strategy the best strategy for you? Not necessarily. But it's a starting point.

25

Putting It All Together

Being a parent is the hardest job on the planet. As a parent, you are going to make mistakes time and time again. You will frequently worry if you are good enough, you will constantly question your parenting techniques, and you will doubt yourself and your abilities time and time again. Worse yet, you will compare yourself to other parents or compare your child to other children. Despite your perceived shortcomings, I challenge you to change your perspective.

This is what I know to be true. "Bad" parents do not ever question their parenting abilities. They are too caught up in their own stuff to care about how they are parenting their kids. If you have ever doubted yourself as a parent, congratulations. That self-doubt indicates that you are concerned enough about the well-being of your child or children that you question your abilities. This alone means that you are a great parent. Please believe that.

Despite my extensive training as a pediatrician, and despite the decades I have spent educating myself about child development and discipline, I am still learning. I make perceived parenting mistakes daily. I frequently doubt myself and my abilities. Why? Because I love my children fiercely, I want the best for them, and I am a human being just like you. My husband will tell you that I am too hard on myself. He insists that I am the most amazing mom that he has ever seen. But my perspective is different. I'm too hard on myself, and I bet you are as well.

Be patient with yourself. Change takes time. The truth is that you are probably going to need to read certain chapters of this book multiple times. Some of the concepts that have been discussed are challenging to process. Please remember, I spent four years in medical school, three years in a residency program working up to eighty hours per week, and have a decade of pediatric medical experience. In addition, I accrue at least twenty hours of continuing education per year in order to improve my medical and parenting skills.

Reading this book once may not completely change your life. I don't expect it to. I understand that if your child is currently five years old, the teenage information does not currently apply to you. I get that. However, reading certain chapters over and over again may make all the difference.

I intended this to be a reference book, not a one-time-and-done book. You may need to come back to certain aspects of this book time and time again. Great! That's exactly what I want for you. The best parenting books that I own are ones that I pull off of my bookshelf every few months, or even once a year. I read a few pages, or maybe even a few chapters, and remind myself of the concepts that apply to my family. My hope is that you use this book and adopt a similar strategy.

Full disclosure: trying to summarize the parenting strategies that will help your child thrive in one chapter is absolutely daunting. I'll do my best.

From the moment your child is born, provide them with unconditional love and affection. Focus on creating a secure and consistent environment for your child. Attend to your infant's needs to the best of your ability. Start reading to your child when they are far too young to understand what you are reading.

Get comfortable with emotions. Commit to expressing your emotions in an appropriate manner, but be patient with yourself—especially if you grew up in a home where emotional expression was not encouraged or accepted. At the same time, commit to accepting and allowing your child to feel what they are feeling. Focus on teaching your child appropriate expression of emotions, rather than trying to tell your children that their feelings are wrong or unacceptable. Remember, emotions are neither good nor bad, and no feeling is final.

Take the time to understand the neurocognitive, emotional, and social development of your child throughout the course of their life. Understand your child's unique temperamental attributes. Use this information to guide your parenting strategies. If this seems overwhelming, I highly recommend that you only focus on material that relates to your child's current stage of development. Incorporate this information into your current parenting strategies. As your child gets older, you'll have plenty of opportunities to pick up this book in the future and continue to learn.

Human behavior is complicated; thoughts, emotions, and actions are intimately related. Remember the concept of modeling, and make sure to act in the way you want your child to act. When your child misbehaves, do your best to stay calm, and put your beautifully developed brain into action in order to think before you react. Do your best to attempt to view the world through your child's eyes. You will be much more effective as a parent if you can understand your child's perspective about the world around them and through the lens of their current abilities.

Finally, be fair and consistent when providing consequences for unwanted behaviors. Make sure that the consequence matches the severity of the transgression. Be sure that you will follow through on implementing that consequence and don't make empty threats. Make sure to explain to your child, in developmentally appropriate terms, why they are receiving the consequence and how they could behave more appropriately in the future.

If that sounds amazingly complex, it is. But it is achievable. Every single interaction that you have with your child provides an opportunity for learning and improvement. Be patient with yourself, and be patient with your child. Life is complicated. It's wonderful, but it can be messy. Parenting another human being is not for the faint of heart. You are going to make mistakes, your child is going to make mistakes, and that is okay. There is no such thing as a perfect parent. But there is such a thing as a loving, understanding, and present parent.

I always tell the families in my pediatric medical practice that the days of a parent are long but the years are short. Enjoy the lovely moments, and trust that the challenging moments will pass. Cherish the hugs and kisses, and don't take the hitting or back talk personally. Finally, be kind to yourself. Acknowledge that your desire to improve your parenting skills means that you have a deep love for your child. You did what you did until you knew how to do better. Now put this book down, give your kids a hug, and tell them how lucky you are to be their parent.

NOTES

Introduction

1 Luther Emmett Holt. *The Care and Feeding of Children*, 8th edn (New York and London: D. Appleton and Company, 1917).

2 John B. Watson, and Rosalie Alberta Rayner Watson. *Psychological Care of Infant and Child*. Family in America (New York: W. W. Norton, 1928).

Chapter 2

1 A. W. Tadesse, B. A. Dachew, G. Ayano, K. Betts, and R. Alati. "Prenatal Cannabis Use and the Risk of Attention Deficit Hyperactivity Disorder and Autism Spectrum Disorder in Offspring: A Systematic Review and Meta-Analysis," *Journal of Psychiatric Research* 171 (March 2024): 142–51. https://doi.org/10.1016/j.jpsychires.2024.01.045

2 Daniel J. Siegel, and Tina Payne Bryson. *The Whole-Brain Child: 12 Revolutionary Strategies to Nurture Your Child's Developing Mind* (New York: Delacorte Press, 2011).

Chapter 5

1 Jean Piaget, 1896–1980. *The Origins of Intelligence in Children* (New York: International Universities Press, 1952).

Chapter 7

1 Daniel Goleman. *Emotional Intelligence* (New York: Bantam Books, 1995).

2 Peter Salovey, and John D. Mayer. "Emotional Intelligence," *Imagination, Cognition and Personality* 9, no. 3 (1990): 185–211.

Chapter 8

1. John Bowlby. *Attachment and Loss: Volume 1: Attachment*, 2nd edn (New York: Basic Books, 1982).

Chapter 10

1. American Psychological Association. "Personality," in *APA Dictionary of Psychology*. Retrieved September 22, 2024 from https://dictionary.apa.org/personality

2. Erik H. Erikson. *Childhood and Society* (New York: W.W. Norton & Company, 1950).

Chapter 11

1. Fred Rogers. "Quotes," *BrainyQuote*. Accessed March 10, 2023. https://www.brainyquote.com/quotes/fred_rogers_193081

2. Mildren Parten. "An Analysis of Social Participation, Leadership, and Other Factors in Preschool Play Groups" (PhD thesis, University of Minnesota, 1929).

Chapter 13

1. Alexander Thomas, and Stella Chess. *Temperament and Development* (New York: Brunner/Mazel, 1977).

Chapter 14

1. Kenneth R. Ginsburg, Martha Moraghan Jablow, and American Academy of Pediatrics. *Building Resilience in Children and Teens: Giving Kids Roots and Wings*, 2nd edn (Elk Grove Village, IL: American Academy of Pediatrics, 2011).

Chapter 17

1. Stephen R. Covey. *The Seven Habits of Highly Effective People: Restoring the Character Ethic* (New York: Simon and Schuster, 1989).

Chapter 18

1. Leon Festinger. "A Theory of Social Comparison Processes," *Human Relations* 7, no. 2 (1954): 117–40. https://doi.org/10.1177/001872675400700202

Chapter 20

1. M. J. MacKenzie, E. Nicklas, J. Waldfogel, and J. Brooks-Gunn. "Spanking and Child Development across the First Decade of Life," *Pediatrics* 132, no. 5 (November 2013): e1118-25.

2. J. Cuartas. "The Effect of Spanking on Early Social-Emotional Skills," *Child Dev* 93, no. 1 (January 2022): 180–93.

Chapter 22

1. Diana Baumrind. "Child Care Practices Anteceding Three Patterns of Preschool Behavior," *Genetic Psychology Monographs* 75, no.1 (1967): 43–88.

2. Miran Lavrič, and Andrej Naterer. "The Power of Authoritative Parenting: A Cross-National Study of Effects of Exposure to Different Parenting Styles on Life Satisfaction," *Children and Youth Services Review* 116 (2020): 105274.

3. H. Masud, M. S. Ahmad, K. W. Cho, and Z. Fakhr. "Parenting Styles and Aggression among Young Adolescents: A Systematic Review of Literature," *Community Ment Health J* 55, no. 6 (August 2019): 1015–30.

BIBLIOGRAPHY

American Psychological Association. (n.d.). "Personality." In *APA Dictionary of Psychology*. Retrieved September 22, 2024 from https://dictionary.apa.org/personality

Bowlby, John. *Attachment and Loss: Volume 1: Attachment*, 2nd edn. New York: Basic Books, 1982.

Covey, Stephen R. *The Seven Habits of Highly Effective People: Restoring the Character Ethic*. New York: Simon and Schuster, 1989.

Cuartas, J. "The Effect of Spanking on Early Social-Emotional Skills." *Child Dev* 93, no. 1 (January 2022): 180–93.

Erikson, Erik H. *Childhood and Society*. New York: W.W. Norton & Company, 1950.

Festinger, Leon. "A Theory of Social Comparison Processes." *Human Relations* 7, no. 2 (1954): 117–40. https://doi.org/10.1177/001872675400700202

Ginsburg, Kenneth R., Martha Moraghan Jablow, and American Academy of Pediatrics. *Building Resilience in Children and Teens: Giving Kids Roots and Wings*, 2nd edn. Elk Grove Village, IL: American Academy of Pediatrics, 2011.

Goleman, Daniel. *Emotional Intelligence*. New York: Bantam Books, 1995.

Holt, Luther Emmett. *The Care and Feeding of Children*, 8th edn. New York and London: D. Appleton and company, 1917.

Lavrič, Miran, and Andrej Naterer. "The Power of Authoritative Parenting: A Cross-National Study of Effects of Exposure to Different Parenting Styles on Life Satisfaction." *Children and Youth Services Review* 116 (2020): 105274.

MacKenzie, M. J., E. Nicklas, J. Waldfogel, and J. Brooks-Gunn. "Spanking and Child Development across the First Decade of Life." *Pediatrics* 132, no. 5 (November 2013): e1118–25.

Masud, H., M. S. Ahmad, K. W. Cho, and Z. Fakhr. "Parenting Styles and Aggression among Young Adolescents: A Systematic Review of Literature." *Community Ment Health J* 55, no. 6 (August 2019): 1015–30.

Parten, Mildred. "An Analysis of Social Participation, Leadership, and Other Factors in Preschool Play Groups." PhD thesis, University of Minnesota, 1929.

Piaget, Jean, 1896–1980. *The Origins of Intelligence in Children*. New York: International Universities Press, 1952.

Rogers, Fred, "Quotes." *BrainyQuote*. Accessed March 10, 2023. https://www.brainyquote.com/quotes/fred_rogers_193081

Salovey, Peter, and John D. Mayer. "Emotional Intelligence." *Imagination, Cognition and Personality* 9, no. 3 (1990): 185–211.

Siegel, Daniel J., and Tina Payne Bryson. *The Whole-Brain Child: 12 Revolutionary Strategies to Nurture Your Child's Developing Mind.* New York: Delacorte Press, 2011.

Tadesse, A. W., B. A. Dachew, G. Ayano, K. Betts, and R. Alati. "Prenatal Cannabis Use and the Risk of Attention Deficit Hyperactivity Disorder and Autism Spectrum Disorder in Offspring: A Systematic Review and Meta-Analysis." *Journal of Psychiatric Research* 171 (March 2024): 142–51. https://doi.org/10.1016/j.jpsychires.2024.01.045

Thomas, Alexander, and Stella Chess. *Temperament and Development.* New York: Brunner/Mazel, 1977.

Watson, John B., and Rosalie Alberta Rayner Watson. *Psychological Care of Infant and Child.* Family in America. New York: W. W. Norton, 1928.

INDEX

accumbens, nucleus   35–7
adolescents, development of   34–8
amygdala   25–30
attachment   75–80
attention span   34
authority, challenging   34–5

behavior
    problematic   28–30
    self-regulation of   33
    understanding and responding
        to   13–30
brain development   17–38
    basics   17–21
    historical context   7–10
    pruning   15, 18
    from toddlers to teenagers   31–8

cognitive development   39–52
colic, infantile   6, 9
control, illusion of parental   4–5
crying   4, 21, 30

development
    emotional   53–80
    neurocognitive   11–52
    psychosocial   81–106
discipline
    age-appropriate   213–24
    effective strategies   179–86
    understanding   171–8

emotional regulation   20–1, 53–6
emotions
    suppression of   55–66
    understanding   55–66
executive functioning   20–2, 34

fight-flight-freeze response   25–30
forebrain   18–21
frontal lobe   20–2, 34

goodness of fit   109–14
guilt, parental   6

impulsivity   21
infanticide   7–8
introduction   1–10

memory
    verbal and nonverbal   20
misbehavior
    interpretation of   4, 27–30
misconceptions about
    parenting   153–60
modeling   83–6

neocortex   19–23
neurocognitive development, *see*
    brain development
neurodiversity   40
neuroplasticity   18

parenting
    historical practices   7–10
    managing guilt   6
    "power moves"   133–68
    societal expectations   5–6
    styles (Baumrind's)   189–200
play–importance in psychosocial
    development   93–8
preschoolers–behavior and brain
    development   31–3
punishment–distinction from
    discipline   5, 179

INDEX

regulation
    emotional 20–1
    self 33
rewards and motivation 35–6

self-awareness 20
sensory development 41
sleep 6, 34
social-emotional development 53–80
societal norms and parenting 5–6
stress 3–4

tantrums 2–3, 28–30, 32–3
teenagers 34–8
temperament
    attributes of 115–26
    understanding 107–14
theory of cognitive development (Piaget) 39–52
thinking skills 34
toddler behavior 2–4, 31–3

values and belief systems in teens 37–8

ABOUT THE AUTHOR

Kristen Cook, MD, is a pediatrician with over a decade of experience in the medical field. She graduated from Creighton University School of Medicine with honors, then completed a challenging residency program at Children's Hospital of Wisconsin. She started her career as a pediatrician in 2010 and remains at that medical practice to this day.

Kristen is happily married to her husband, Chad. Along with their children, Mason and Savannah, they live in the northern suburbs of Chicago. Dr. Cook loves to connect with other parents. You can find her on TikTok and Instagram at momdoctalk_kcmd.